YOUR PERSONAL HOROSCOPE 2018

ARIES

Your Personal Horoscope 2018

Aries

21st March–20th April

igloobooks

Published in 2017
by Igloo Books Ltd
Cottage Farm
Sywell
NN6 0BJ
www.igloobooks.com

Produced for Igloo Books by Foulsham Publishing Ltd, The Old Barrel Store,
Drayman's Lane, Marlow, Bucks SL7 2FF, England

FIR003 0717
2 4 6 8 10 9 7 5 3 1
ISBN: 978-1-78670-877-9

This is an abridged version of material originally published
in Old Moore's Horoscope and Astral Diary.

Cover design by Charles Wood-Penn
Edited by Jasmin Peppiatt

Printed and manufactured in China

CONTENTS

INTRODUCTION

Your Personal Horoscopes have been specifically created to allow you to get the most from astrological patterns and the way they have a bearing on not only your zodiac sign, but nuances within it. Using the diary section of the book you can read about the influences and possibilities of each and every day of the year. It will be possible for you to see when you are likely to be cheerful and happy or those times when your nature is in retreat and you will be more circumspect. The diary will help to give you a feel for the specific 'cycles' of astrology and the way they can subtly change your day-to-day life. For example, when you see the sign ☿, this means that the planet Mercury is retrograde at that time. Retrograde means it appears to be running backwards through the zodiac. Such a happening has a significant effect on communication skills, but this is only one small aspect of how the Personal Horoscope can help you.

With Your Personal Horoscope the story doesn't end with the diary pages. It includes simple ways for you to work out the zodiac sign the Moon occupied at the time of your birth, and what this means for your personality. In addition, if you know the time of day you were born, it is possible to discover your Ascendant, yet another important guide to your personal make-up and potential.

Many readers are interested in relationships and in knowing how well they get on with people of other astrological signs. You might also be interested in the way you appear to very different sorts of individuals. If you are such a person, the section on Venus will be of particular interest. Despite the rapidly changing position of this planet, you can work out your Venus sign, and learn what bearing it will have on your life.

Using Your Personal Horoscope you can travel on one of the most fascinating and rewarding journeys that anyone can take – the journey to a better realisation of self.

THE ESSENCE OF ARIES

Exploring the Personality of Aries the Ram

(21ST MARCH – 20TH APRIL)

What's in a sign?

Aries is not the first sign of the zodiac by accident. It's the place in the year when the spring begins, and so it represents some of the most dynamic forces in nature, and within the zodiac as a whole. As a result the very essence of your nature is geared towards promoting yourself in life and pushing your ideas forward very positively. You don't brook a great deal of interference in your life, but you are quite willing to help others as much as you can, provided that to do so doesn't curb your natural desire to get on in life.

Aries people are not universally liked, though your true friends remain loyal to you under almost any circumstances. But why should it be that such a dynamic and go-getting person does meet with some opposition? The answer is simple: not everyone is quite so sure of themselves as you are and many tend to get nervous when faced with the sheer power of the Aries personality. If there is one factor within your own control that could counter these problems it is the adoption of some humility – that commodity which is so important for you to dredge from the depths of your nature. If you only show the world that you are human, and that you are well aware of the fact, most people would follow you willingly to the very gates of hell. The most successful Aries subjects know this fact and cultivate it to the full.

Your executive skills are never in doubt and you can get almost anything practical done whilst others are still jumping from foot to foot. That's why you are such a good organiser and are so likely to be out there at the front of any venture. Adventurous and quite willing to show your bravery in public, you can even surprise yourself sometimes with the limits you are likely to go to in order to reach solutions that seem right to you.

Kind to those you take to, you can be universally loved when working at your best. Despite this there will be times in your life when you simply can't understand why some people just don't like you. Maybe there's an element of jealousy involved.

Aries resources

The part of the zodiac occupied by the sign of Aries has, for many centuries, been recognised as the home of self-awareness. This means that there isn't a person anywhere else in the zodiac that has a better knowledge of self than you do. But this isn't necessarily an intellectual process with Aries, more a response to the very blood that is coursing through your veins. Aries' success doesn't so much come from spending hours working out the pros and cons of any given course of action, more from the thrill of actually getting stuck in. If you find yourself forced into a life that means constantly having to think everything through to the tiniest detail, there is likely to be some frustration in evidence.

Aries is ruled by Mars, arguably the most go-getting of all the planets in the solar system. Mars is martial and demands practical ways of expressing latent power. It also requires absolute obedience from subordinates. When this is forthcoming, Aries individuals are the most magnanimous people to be found anywhere. Loyalty is not a problem and there have been many instances in history when Aries people were quite willing to die for their friends if necessary.

When other people are willing to give up and go with the flow, you will still be out there pitching for the result that seems most advantageous to you. It isn't something you can particularly control and those who don't know you well could find you sometimes curt and over-demanding as a result. But because you are tenacious you can pick the bones out of any situation and will usually arrive at your desired destination, if you don't collapse with fatigue on the way.

Routines, or having to take life at the pace of less motivated types, won't suit you at all. Imprisonment of any sort, even in a failed relationship, is sheer torture and you will move heaven and earth to get out into the big, wide world, where you can exploit your natural potential to the full. Few people know you really well because you don't always explain yourself adequately. The ones who do adore you.

Beneath the surface

Whereas some zodiac signs are likely to spend a great deal of their lives looking carefully at the innermost recesses of their own minds, Aries individuals tend to prefer the cut and thrust of the practical world. Aries people are not natural philosophers, but that doesn't mean that you aren't just as complicated beneath the surface as any of your astrological brothers and sisters. So what is it that makes the Aries firebrand think and act in the way that it does? To a great extent it is a lack of basic self-confidence.

This statement might seem rather odd, bearing in mind that a fair percentage of the people running our world were born under the sign of the Ram, but it is true nevertheless. Why? Because people who know themselves and their capabilities really well don't feel the constant need to prove themselves in the way that is the driving force of your zodiac sign. Not that your naturally progressive tendencies are a fault. On the contrary, if used correctly they can help you to create a much better, fairer and happier world, at least in your own vicinity.

The fact that you occasionally take your ball and go home if you can't get your own way is really down to the same insecurity that is noticeable through many facets of your nature. If Aries can't rule, it often doesn't want to play at all. A deep resentment and a brooding quality can build up in the minds and souls of some thwarted Aries types, a tendency that you need to combat. Better by far to try and compromise, itself a word that doesn't exist in the vocabularies of the least enlightened people born under the sign of the Ram. Once this lesson is learned, inner happiness increases and you relax into your life much more.

The way you think about others is directly related to the way you consider they think about you. This leads to another surprising fact regarding the zodiac sign. Aries people absolutely hate to be disliked, though they would move heaven and earth to prove that this isn't the case. And as a result Aries both loves and hates with a passion. Deep inside you can sometimes be a child shivering in the dark. If you only realise this fact your path to happiness and success is almost assured. Of course to do so takes a good deal of courage – but that's a commodity you don't lack.

Making the best of yourself

It would be quite clear to any observer that you are not the sort of person who likes to hang around at the back of a queue, or who would relish constantly taking orders from people who may not know situations as well as you do. For that reason alone you are better in positions that see you out there at the front, giving commands and enjoying the cut and thrust of everyday life. In a career sense this means that whatever you do you are happiest telling those around you how to do it too. Many Aries people quite naturally find their way to the top of the tree and don't usually have too much trouble staying there.

It is important to remember, however, that there is another side to your nature: the giving qualities beneath your natural dominance. You can always be around when people need you the most, encouraging and even gently pushing when it is necessary. By keeping friends and being willing to nurture relationships across a broad spectrum, you gradually get to know what makes those around you tick. This makes for a more patient and understanding sort of Aries subject – the most potent of all.

Even your resilience is not endless, which is why it is important to remember that there are times when you need rest. Bearing in mind that you are not superhuman is the hardest lesson to learn, but the admission brings humility, something that Aries needs to cultivate whenever possible.

Try to avoid living a restricted life and make your social contacts frequent and important. Realise that there is much more to life than work and spend some of your free time genuinely attempting to help those who are less well off than you are. Crucially you must remember that 'help' is not the same as domination.

The impressions you give

This section may well be of less interest to Aries subjects than it would be to certain other zodiac signs. The reason is quite clear. Aries people are far less interested in what others think about them than almost anyone else – or at least they tell themselves that they are. Either way it is counterproductive to ignore the opinions of the world at large because to do so creates stumbling blocks, even in a practical sense.

Those around you probably find you extremely capable and well able to deal with almost any situation that comes your way. Most are willing to rely heavily on you and the majority would almost instinctively see you as a leader. Whether or not they like you at the same time is really dependent on the way you handle situations. That's the difference between the go-getting, sometimes selfish type of Aries subject and the more enlightened amongst this illustrious sign.

You are viewed as being exciting and well able to raise enthusiasm for almost any project that takes your fancy. Of course this implies a great responsibility because you are always expected to come up with the goods. The world tends to put certain people on a pedestal, and you are one of them. On the other side of the coin we are all inclined to fire arrows at the elevated, so maintaining your position isn't very easy.

Most of the time you are seen as being magnanimous and kind, factors that you can exploit, whilst at the same time recognising the depth of the responsibility that comes with being an Aries subject. It might not be a bad thing to allow those around you to see that you too have feet of clay. This will make them respect and support you all the more, and even Aries people really do need to feel loved. A well-balanced Aries subject is one of the most elevated spirits to be found anywhere.

The way forward

You certainly enjoy life more when looking at it from the top of the tree. Struggling to get by is not in the least interesting to your zodiac sign and you can soon become miserable if things are not going well for you. That's why it is probably quite justified in your case to work tenaciously in order to achieve your objectives. Ideally, once you have realised some sort of success and security for yourself, you should then be willing to sit and watch life go by a little more. In fact this doesn't happen. The reason for this is clear. The Aries subject who learns how to succeed rarely knows when to stop – it's as simple as that.

Splitting your life into different components can help, if only because this means that you don't get the various elements mixed up. So, for example, don't confuse your love life with your professional needs, or your family with colleagues. This process allows you to view life in manageable chunks and also makes it possible for you to realise when any one of them may not be working well. As a result you will put the effort where it's needed, and enjoy what is going well for you.

If you want to know real happiness you will also have to learn that acquisition for its own sake brings hollow rewards at best. When your talents are being turned outward to the world at large, you are one of the most potent and successful people around. What is more you should find yourself to be a much happier person when you are lending a hand to the wider world. This is possible, maybe outside of your normal professional sphere, though even where voluntary work is concerned it is important not to push yourself to the point of fatigue.

Keep yourself physically fit, without necessarily expecting that you can run to the South Pole and back, and stay away from too many stimulants, such as alcohol and nicotine. The fact is that you are best when living a healthy life, but it doesn't help either if you make even abstinence into an art form. Balance is important, as is moderation – itself a word that is difficult for you to understand. In terms of your approach to other people it's important to realise that everyone has a specific point of view. These might be different to yours, but they are not necessarily wrong. Sort out the friends who are most important to you and stick with them, whilst at the same time realising that almost everyone can be a pal – with just a little effort.

ARIES ON THE CUSP

Astrological profiles are altered for those people born at either the beginning or the end of a zodiac sign, or, more properly, on the cusps of a sign. In the case of Aries this would be on the 21st of March and for two or three days after, and similarly at the end of the sign, probably from the 18th to the 20th of April.

The Pisces Cusp – March 21st to March 24th

With the Sun so close to the zodiac sign of Pisces at the time you were born, it is distinctly possible that you have always had some doubts when reading a character breakdown written specifically for the sign of Aries. This isn't surprising because no zodiac sign has a definite start or end, they merely merge together. As a result there are some of the characteristics of the sign of the Fishes that are intermingled with the qualities of Aries in your nature.

What we probably find, as a result, is a greater degree of emotional sensitivity and a tendency to be more cognisant of what the rest of humanity is feeling. This is not to imply that Aries is unfeeling, but rather that Pisceans actively make humanity their business.

You are still able to achieve your most desired objectives in the practical world, but on the way, you stop to listen to the heartbeat of the planet on which you live. A very good thing, of course, but at the same time there is some conflict created if your slightly dream-like tendencies get in the way of your absolute need to see things through to their logical conclusion.

Nobody knows you better than you know yourself, or at least that's what the Aries qualities within you say, but that isn't always verified by some of the self-doubt that comes from the direction of the Fishes. As in all matters astrological, a position of balance has to be achieved in order to reconcile the differing qualities of your nature. In your case, this is best accomplished by being willing to stop and think once in a while and by refusing to allow your depth to be a problem.

Dealt with properly, the conjoining of Pisces and Aries can be a wondrous and joyful affair, a harmony of opposites that always makes you interesting to know. Your position in the world is naturally one of authority but at the same time you need to serve. That's why some people with this sort of mixture of astrological qualities would make such good administrators in a hospital, or in any position where the alternate astrological needs are well balanced. In the chocolate box of life you are certainly a 'soft centre'.

The Taurus Cusp – April 18th to April 20th

The merge from Aries to Taurus is much less well defined than the one at the other side of Aries, but it can be very useful to you all the same. Like the Pisces-influenced Aries you may be slightly more quiet than would be the case with the Ram taken alone and your thought processes are probably not quite as fast. But to compensate for this fact you don't rush into things quite as much and are willing to allow ideas to mature more fully.

Your sense of harmony and beauty is strong and you know, in a very definite way, exactly what you want. As a result your home will be distinctive but tasteful and it's a place where you need space to be alone sometimes, which the true Aries subject probably does not. You do not lack the confidence to make things look the way you want them, but you have a need to display these things to the world at large and sometimes even to talk about how good you are at decoration and design.

If anyone finds you pushy, it is probably because they don't really know what makes you tick. Although you are willing to mix with almost anyone, you are more inclined, at base, to have a few very close friends who stay at the forefront of your life for a long time. It is likely that you enjoy refined company and you wouldn't take kindly to the dark, the sordid, or the downright crude in life.

Things don't get you down as much as can sometimes be seen to be the case for Taurus when taken alone and you are rarely stumped for a progressive and practical idea when one is needed most. At all levels, your creative energy is evident and some of you even have the ability to make this into a business, since Aries offers the practical and administrative spark that Taurus can sometimes lack.

In matters of love, you are ardent and sincere, probably an idealist, and you know what you want in a partner. Whilst this is also true in the case of Taurus, you are different, because you are much more likely, not only to look, but also to say something about the way you feel.

Being naturally friendly you rarely go short of the right sort of help and support when it is most vital. Part of the reason for this lies in the fact that you are so willing to be the sounding-board for the concerns of your friends. All in all you can be very contented with your lot, but you never stop searching for something better all the same. At its best, this is one of the most progressive cuspal matches of them all.

ARIES AND ITS ASCENDANTS

The nature of every individual on the planet is composed of the rich variety of zodiac signs and planetary positions that were present at the time of their birth. Your Sun sign, which in your case is Aries, is one of the many factors when it comes to assessing the unique person you are. Probably the most important consideration, other than your Sun sign, is to establish the zodiac sign that was rising over the eastern horizon at the time that you were born. This is your Ascending or Rising sign. Most popular astrology fails to take account of the Ascendant, and yet its importance remains with you from the very moment of your birth, through every day of your life. The Ascendant is evident in the way you approach the world, and so, when meeting a person for the first time, it is this astrological influence that you are most likely to notice first. Our Ascending sign essentially represents what we appear to be, while our Sun sign is what we feel inside ourselves.

The Ascendant also has the potential for modifying our overall nature. For example, if you were born at a time of day when Aries was passing over the eastern horizon (this would be around the time of dawn) then you would be classed as a double Aries. As such you would typify this zodiac sign, both internally and in your dealings with others. However, if your Ascendant sign turned out to be a Water sign, such as Pisces, there would be a profound alteration of nature, away from the expected qualities of Aries.

One of the reasons that popular astrology often ignores the Ascendant is that it has always been rather difficult to establish. We have found a way to make this possible by devising an easy-to-use table, which you will find on page 157 of this book. Using this, you can establish your Ascendant sign at a glance. You will need to know your rough time of birth, then it is simply a case of following the instructions.

For those readers who have no idea of their time of birth it might be worth allowing a good friend, or perhaps your partner, to read through the section that follows this introduction. Someone who deals with you on a regular basis may easily discover your Ascending sign, even though you could have some difficulty establishing it for yourself. A good understanding of this component of your nature is essential if you want to be aware of that 'other person' who is responsible for the way you make contact with the world at large. Your Sun sign, Ascendant sign, and the other pointers in this book will, together, allow you a far better understanding of what makes you tick as an individual. Peeling back the different layers of your astrological make-up can be an enlightening experience, and the Ascendant may represent one of the most important layers of all.

Aries with Aries Ascendant

What you see is what you get with this combination. You typify the no-nonsense approach of Aries at its best. All the same this combination is quite daunting when viewed through the eyes of other, less dominant sorts of people. You tend to push your way though situations that would find others cowering in a corner and you are afraid of very little. With a determination to succeed that makes you a force to be reckoned with, you leave the world in no doubt as to your intentions and tend to be rather too brusque for your own good on occasions.

At heart you are kind and loving, able to offer assistance to the downtrodden and sad, and usually willing to take on board the cares of people who have a part to play in your life. No-one would doubt your sincerity, or your honesty, though you may utilise slightly less than orthodox ways of getting your own way on those occasions when you feel you have right on your side. You are a loving partner and a good parent, though where children are concerned you tend to be rather too protective. The trouble is that you know what a big, bad world it can be and probably feel that you are better equipped to deal with things than anyone else.

Aries with Taurus Ascendant

This is a much quieter combination, so much so that even experienced astrologers would be unlikely to recognise you as an Aries subject at all, unless of course they came to know you very well. Your approach to life tends to be quiet and considered and there is a great danger that you could suppress those feelings that others of your kind would be only too willing to verbalise. To compensate you are deeply creative and will think matters through much more readily than more dominant Aries types would be inclined to do. Reaching out towards the world, you are, nevertheless, somewhat locked inside yourself and can struggle to achieve the level of communication that you so desperately need. Frustration might easily follow, were it not for the fact that you possess a quiet determination that, to those in the know, is the clearest window through to your Aries soul.

The care for others is stronger here than with almost any other Aries type and you certainly demonstrate this at all levels. The fact is that you live a great percentage of your life in service to the people you take to, whilst at the same time being able to shut the door firmly in the face of people who irritate or anger you. You are deeply motivated towards family relationships.

Aries with Gemini Ascendant

A fairly jolly combination this, though by no means easy for others to come to terms with. You fly about from pillar to post and rarely stop long enough to take a breath. Admittedly this suits your own needs very well, but it can be a source of some disquiet to those around you, since they may not possess your energy or motivation. Those who know you well are deeply in awe of your capacity to keep going long after almost everyone else would have given up and gone home, though this quality is not always as wonderful as it sounds because it means that you put more pressure on your nervous system than just about any other astrological combination.

You need to be mindful of your nervous system, which responds to the erratic, mercurial quality of Gemini. Problems only really arise when the Aries part of you makes demands that the Gemini component finds difficult to deal with. There are paradoxes galore here and some of them need sorting out if you are ever fully to understand yourself, or are to be in a position when others know what makes you tick.

In relationships you might be a little fickle, but you are a real charmer and never stuck for the right words, no matter who you are dealing with. Your tenacity knows no bounds, though perhaps it should!

Aries with Cancer Ascendant

The main problem that you experience in life shows itself as a direct result of the meshing of these two very different zodiac signs. At heart Aries needs to dominate, whereas Cancer shows a desire to nurture. All too often the result can be a protective arm that is so strong that nobody could possibly get out from under it. Lighten your own load, and that of those you care for, by being willing to sit back and watch others please themselves a little. You might think that you know best, and your heart is clearly in the right place, but try to realise what life is like when someone is always on hand to tell you that they know better then you do.

But in a way this is a little severe, because you are fairly intuitive and your instincts would rarely lead you astray. Nobody could ask for a better partner or parent than you, though they might request a slightly less attentive one. In matters of work you are conscientious and are probably best suited to a job that means sorting out the kind of mess that humanity is so good at creating. You probably spend your spare time untangling balls of wool, though you are quite sporting too and could easily make the Olympics. Once there you would not win however, because you would be too concerned about all the other competitors.

Aries with Leo Ascendant

Here we come upon the first situation of Aries being allied with another Fire sign. This creates a character that could appear to be typically Aries at first sight and in many ways it is, though there are subtle differences that should not be ignored. Although you have the typical Aries ability to get things done, many of the tasks you do undertake will be for and on behalf of others. You can be proud, and on some occasions even haughty, and yet you are also regal in your bearing and honest to the point of absurdity. Nobody could doubt your sincerity and you have the soul of a poet combined with the courage of a lion.

All this is good, but it makes you rather difficult to approach, unless the person in question has first adopted a crouching and subservient attitude although you would not wish them to do so. It's simply that the impression you give and the motivation that underpins it are two quite different things. You are greatly respected and in the case of those individuals who know your real nature, you are also deeply loved. But life would be much simpler if you didn't always have to fight the wars that those around you are happy to start. Relaxation is a word that you don't really understand and you would do yourself a favour if you looked it up in a dictionary.

Aries with Virgo Ascendant

Virgo is steady and sure, though also fussy and stubborn. Aries is fast and determined, restless and active. It can already be seen that this is a rather strange meeting of characteristics and because Virgo is ruled by the capricious Mercury, the ultimate result will change from hour to hour and day to day. It isn't merely that others find it difficult to know where they are with you, they can't even understand what makes you tick. This will make you the subject of endless fascination and attention, at which you will be apparently surprised but inwardly pleased. If anyone ever really gets to know what goes on in that busy mind they may find the implications very difficult to deal with and it is a fact that only you would have the ability to live inside your crowded head.

As a partner and a parent you are second to none, though you tend to get on better with your children once they start to grow, since by this time you may be slightly less restricting to their own desires, which will often clash with your own on their behalf. You are capable of give and take and could certainly not be considered selfish, though your constant desire to get the best from everyone might occasionally be misconstrued.

Aries with Libra Ascendant

Libra has the tendency to bring out the best in any zodiac sign, and this is no exception when it comes together with Aries. You may, in fact, be the most comfortable of all Aries types, simply because Libra tempers some of your more assertive qualities and gives you the chance to balance out opposing forces, both inside yourself and in the world outside. You are fun to be with and make the staunchest friend possible. Although you are generally affable, few people would try to put one over on you, because they would quickly come to know how far you are willing to go before you let forth a string of invective that would shock those who previously underestimated your basic Aries traits.

Home and family are very dear to you, but you are more tolerant than some Aries types are inclined to be and you have a youthful zest for life that should stay with you no matter what age you manage to achieve. There is always something interesting to do and your mind is a constant stream of possibilities. This makes you very creative and you may also demonstrate a desire to look good at all times. You may not always be quite as confident as you appear to be, but few would guess the fact.

Aries with Scorpio Ascendant

The two very different faces of Mars come together in this potent, magnetic and quite awe-inspiring combination. Your natural inclination is towards secrecy and this fact, together with the natural attractions of the sensual Scorpio nature, makes you the object of great curiosity. This means that you will not go short of attention and should ensure that you are always being analysed by people who may never get to know you at all. At heart you prefer your own company, and yet life appears to find means to push you into the public gaze time and again. Most people with this combination ooze sex appeal and can use this fact as a stepping stone to personal success, yet without losing any integrity or loosening the cords of a deeply moralistic nature.

On those occasions when you do lose your temper, there isn't a character in the length and breadth of the zodiac who would have either the words or the courage to stand against the stream of invective that follows. On really rare occasions you might even scare yourself. As far as family members are concerned a simple look should be enough to show when you are not amused. Few people are left unmoved by your presence in their life.

Aries with Sagittarius Ascendant

What a lovely combination this can be, for the devil-may-care aspects of Sagittarius lighten the load of a sometimes too-serious Aries interior. Everything that glistens is not gold, though it's hard to convince you of the fact because, to mix metaphors, you can make a silk purse out of a sow's ear. Almost everyone loves you and in return you offer a friendship that is warm and protective, but not as demanding as sometimes tends to be the case with the Aries type. Relationships may be many and varied and there is often more than one major attachment in the life of those holding this combination. You will bring a breath of spring to any attachment, though you need to ensure that the person concerned is capable of keeping up with the hectic pace of your life.

It may appear from time to time that you are rather too trusting for your own good, though deep inside you are very astute and it seems that almost everything you undertake works out well in the end. This has nothing to do with native luck and is really down to the fact that you are much more calculating than might appear to be the case at first sight. As a parent you are protective yet offer sufficient room for self-expression.

Aries with Capricorn Ascendant

If ever anyone could be accused of setting off immediately, but slowly, it has to be you. These are very contradictory signs and the differences will express themselves in a variety of ways. One thing is certain, you have tremendous tenacity and will see a job through patiently from beginning to end, without tiring on the way, and ensuring that every detail is taken care of properly. This combination often bestows good health and a great capacity for continuity, particularly in terms of the length of life. You are certainly not as argumentative as the typical Aries, but you do know how to get your own way, which is just as well because you are usually thinking on behalf of everyone else and not just on your own account.

At home you can relax, which is a blessing for Aries, though in fact you seldom choose to do so because you always have some project or other on the go. You probably enjoy knocking down and rebuilding walls, though this is a practical tendency and not responsive to relationships, in which you are ardent and sincere. Impetuosity is as close to your heart as is the case for any type of Aries subject, though you certainly have the ability to appear patient and steady. But it's just a front, isn't it?

Aries with Aquarius Ascendant

The person standing on a soap box in the corner of the park, extolling the virtues of this or that, could quite easily be an Aries with an Aquarian Ascendant. You are certainly not averse to speaking your mind and you have plenty to talk about because you are the best social reformer and political animal of them all. Unorthodox in your approach, you have the ability to keep everyone guessing, except when it comes to getting your own way, for in this nobody doubts your natural abilities. You can put theories into practice very well and on the way you retain a sense of individuality that would shock more conservative types. It's true that a few people might find you a little difficult to approach and this is partly because you have an inner reserve and strength which is difficult for others to fathom.

In the world at large you take your place at the front, as any good Arian should, and yet you offer room for others to share your platform. You keep up with the latest innovations and treat family members as the genuine friends that you believe them to be. Care needs to be taken when picking a life partner, for you are an original, and not just anyone could match the peculiarities thrown up by this astrological combination.

Aries with Pisces Ascendant

Although not an easy combination to deal with, the Aries with a Piscean Ascendant does, nevertheless, bring something very special to the world in the way of natural understanding allied to practical assistance. It's true that you can sometimes be a dreamer, but there is nothing wrong with that as long as you have the ability to turn some of your wishes into reality, and this you are easily able to do, usually for the sake of those around you. Conversation comes easily to you, though you also possess a slightly wistful and poetic side to your nature, which is attractive to the many people who call you a friend. A natural entertainer, you bring a sense of the comic to the often serious qualities of Aries, though without losing the determination that typifies the sign.

In relationships you are ardent, sincere and supportive, with a strong social conscience that sometimes finds you fighting the battles of the less privileged members of society. Family is important to you and this is a combination that invariably leads to parenthood. Away from the cut and thrust of everyday life you relax more fully and think about matters more deeply than more typical Aries types might.

THE MOON AND THE PART IT PLAYS IN YOUR LIFE

In astrology the Moon is probably the single most important heavenly body after the Sun. Its unique position, as partner to the Earth on its journey around the solar system, means that the Moon appears to pass through the signs of the zodiac extremely quickly. The zodiac position of the Moon at the time of your birth plays a great part in personal character and is especially significant in the build-up of your emotional nature.

Your Own Moon Sign

Discovering the position of the Moon at the time of your birth has always been notoriously difficult because tracking the complex zodiac positions of the Moon is not easy. This process has been reduced to three simple stages with our Lunar Tables. A breakdown of the Moon's zodiac positions can be found from page 35 onwards, so that once you know what your Moon Sign is, you can see what part this plays in the overall build-up of your personal character.

If you follow the instructions on the next page you will soon be able to work out exactly what zodiac sign the Moon occupied on the day that you were born and you can then go on to compare the reading for this position with those of your Sun sign and your Ascendant. It is partly the comparison between these three important positions that goes towards making you the unique individual you are.

HOW TO DISCOVER YOUR MOON SIGN

This is a three-stage process. You may need a pen and a piece of paper but if you follow the instructions below the process should only take a minute or so.

STAGE 1 First of all you need to know the Moon Age at the time of your birth. If you look at Moon Table 1, on page 33, you will find all the years between 1920 and 2018 down the left side. Find the year of your birth and then trace across to the right to the month of your birth. Where the two intersect you will find a number. This is the date of the New Moon in the month that you were born. You now need to count forward the number of days between the New Moon and your own birthday. For example, if the New Moon in the month of your birth was shown as being the 6th and you were born on the 20th, your Moon Age Day would be 14. If the New Moon in the month of your birth came after your birthday, you need to count forward from the New Moon in the previous month. If you were born in a Leap Year, remember to count the 29th February. You can tell if your birth year was a Leap Year if the last two digits can be divided by four. Whatever the result, jot this number down so that you do not forget it.

STAGE 2 Take a look at Moon Table 2 on page 34. Down the left hand column look for the date of your birth. Now trace across to the month of your birth. Where the two meet you will find a letter. Copy this letter down alongside your Moon Age Day.

STAGE 3 Moon Table 3 on page 34 will supply you with the zodiac sign the Moon occupied on the day of your birth. Look for your Moon Age Day down the left hand column and then for the letter you found in Stage 2. Where the two converge you will find a zodiac sign and this is the sign occupied by the Moon on the day that you were born.

Your Zodiac Moon Sign Explained

You will find a profile of all zodiac Moon Signs on pages 35 to 38, showing in yet another way how astrology helps to make you into the individual that you are. In each daily entry of the Astral Diary you can find the zodiac position of the Moon for every day of the year. This also allows you to discover your lunar birthdays. Since the Moon passes through all the signs of the zodiac in about a month, you can expect something like twelve lunar birthdays each year. At these times you are likely to be emotionally steady and able to make the sort of decisions that have real, lasting value.

MOON TABLE 1

YEAR	FEB	MAR	APR	YEAR	FEB	MAR	APR	YEAR	FEB	MAR	APR
1920	19	20	18	1953	14	15	13	1986	9	10	9
1921	8	9	8	1954	3	5	3	1987	28	29	28
1922	26	28	27	1955	22	24	22	1988	17	18	16
1923	15	17	16	1956	11	12	11	1989	6	7	6
1924	5	5	4	1957	–	1/31	29	1990	25	26	25
1925	23	24	23	1958	18	20	19	1991	14	15	13
1926	12	14	12	1959	7	9	8	1992	3	4	3
1927	2	3	2	1960	26	27	26	1993	22	24	22
1928	19	21	20	1961	15	16	15	1994	10	12	11
1929	9	11	9	1962	5	6	5	1995	29	30	29
1930	28	30	28	1963	23	25	23	1996	18	19	18
1931	17	19	18	1964	13	14	12	1997	7	9	7
1932	6	7	6	1965	1	2	1	1998	26	27	26
1933	24	26	24	1966	19	21	20	1999	16	17	16
1934	14	15	13	1967	9	10	9	2000	5	6	4
1935	3	5	3	1968	28	29	28	2001	23	24	23
1936	22	23	21	1969	17	18	16	2002	12	13	12
1937	11	13	12	1970	6	7	6	2003	–	2	1
1938	–	2/31	30	1971	25	26	25	2004	20	21	19
1939	19	20	19	1972	14	15	13	2005	9	10	8
1940	8	9	7	1973	4	5	3	2006	28	29	27
1941	26	27	26	1974	22	24	22	2007	15	18	17
1942	15	16	15	1975	11	12	11	2008	6	7	6
1943	4	6	4	1976	29	30	29	2009	25	26	25
1944	24	24	22	1977	18	19	18	2010	14	15	14
1945	12	14	12	1978	7	9	7	2011	3	5	3
1946	2	3	2	1979	26	27	26	2012	22	22	21
1947	19	21	20	1980	15	16	15	2013	10	12	10
1948	9	11	9	1981	4	6	4	2014	1	1/31	30
1949	27	29	28	1982	23	24	23	2015	19	20	19
1950	16	18	17	1983	13	14	13	2016	8	8	7
1951	6	7	6	1984	1	2	1	2017	25	27	25
1952	25	25	24	1985	19	21	20	2018	15	17	16

TABLE 2   MOON TABLE 3

DAY	MAR	APR	M/D	F	G	H	I	J	K	L
1	F	J	0	PI	PI	AR	AR	AR	TA	TA
2	G	J	1	PI	AR	AR	AR	TA	TA	TA
3	G	J	2	AR	AR	AR	TA	TA	TA	GE
4	G	J	3	AR	AR	TA	TA	TA	GE	GE
5	G	J	4	AR	TA	TA	GE	GE	GE	GE
6	G	J	5	TA	TA	GE	GE	GE	CA	CA
7	G	J	6	TA	GE	GE	GE	CA	CA	CA
8	G	J	7	GE	GE	GE	CA	CA	CA	LE
9	G	J	8	GE	GE	CA	CA	CA	LE	LE
10	G	J	9	CA	CA	CA	CA	LE	LE	VI
11	G	K	10	CA	CA	LE	LE	LE	VI	VI
12	H	K	11	CA	LE	LE	LE	VI	VI	VI
13	H	K	12	LE	LE	LE	VI	VI	VI	LI
14	H	K	13	LE	LE	VI	VI	VI	LI	LI
15	H	K	14	VI	VI	VI	LI	LI	LI	LI
16	H	K	15	VI	VI	LI	LI	LI	SC	SC
17	H	K	16	VI	LI	LI	LI	SC	SC	SC
18	H	K	17	LI	LI	LI	SC	SC	SC	SA
19	H	K	18	LI	LI	SC	SC	SC	SA	SA
20	H	K	19	LI	SC	SC	SC	SA	SA	SA
21	H	L	20	SC	SC	SA	SA	SA	CP	CP
22	I	L	21	SC	SA	SA	SA	CP	CP	CP
23	I	L	22	SC	SA	SA	CP	CP	CP	AQ
24	I	L	23	SA	SA	CP	CP	CP	AQ	AQ
25	I	L	24	SA	CP	CP	CP	AQ	AQ	AQ
26	I	L	25	CP	CP	AQ	AQ	AQ	PI	PI
27	I	L	26	CP	AQ	AQ	AQ	PI	PI	PI
28	I	L	27	AQ	AQ	AQ	PI	PI	PI	AR
29	I	L	28	AQ	AQ	PI	PI	PI	AR	AR
30	I	L	29	AQ	PI	PI	PI	AR	AR	AR
31	I	–								

AR = Aries, TA = Taurus, GE = Gemini, CA = Cancer, LE = Leo, VI = Virgo, LI = Libra, SC = Scorpio, SA = Sagittarius, CP = Capricorn, AQ = Aquarius, PI = Pisces

MOON SIGNS

Moon in Aries

You have a strong imagination, courage, determination and a desire to do things in your own way and forge your own path through life.

Originality is a key attribute; you are seldom stuck for ideas although your mind is changeable and you could take the time to focus on individual tasks. Often quick-tempered, you take orders from few people and live life at a fast pace. Avoid health problems by taking regular time out for rest and relaxation.

Emotionally, it is important that you talk to those you are closest to and work out your true feelings. Once you discover that people are there to help, there is less necessity for you to do everything yourself.

Moon in Taurus

The Moon in Taurus gives you a courteous and friendly manner, which means you are likely to have many friends.

The good things in life mean a lot to you, as Taurus is an Earth sign that delights in experiences which please the senses. Hence you are probably a lover of good food and drink, which may in turn mean you need to keep an eye on the bathroom scales, especially as looking good is also important to you.

Emotionally you are fairly stable and you stick by your own standards. Taureans do not respond well to change. Intuition also plays an important part in your life.

Moon in Gemini

You have a warm-hearted character, sympathetic and eager to help others. At times reserved, you can also be articulate and chatty: this is part of the paradox of Gemini, which always brings duplicity to the nature. You are interested in current affairs, have a good intellect, and are good company and likely to have many friends. Most of your friends have a high opinion of you and would be ready to defend you should the need arise. However, this is usually unnecessary, as you are quite capable of defending yourself in any verbal confrontation.

Travel is important to your inquisitive mind and you find intellectual stimulus in mixing with people from different cultures. You also gain much from reading, writing and the arts but you do need plenty of rest and relaxation in order to avoid fatigue.

Moon in Cancer

The Moon in Cancer at the time of birth is a fortunate position as Cancer is the Moon's natural home. This means that the qualities of compassion and understanding given by the Moon are especially enhanced in your nature, and you are friendly and sociable and cope well with emotional pressures. You cherish home and family life, and happily do the domestic tasks. Your surroundings are important to you and you hate squalor and filth. You are likely to have a love of music and poetry.

Your basic character, although at times changeable like the Moon itself, depends on symmetry. You aim to make your surroundings comfortable and harmonious, for yourself and those close to you.

Moon in Leo

The best qualities of the Moon and Leo come together to make you warm-hearted, fair, ambitious and self-confident. With good organisational abilities, you invariably rise to a position of responsibility in your chosen career. This is fortunate as you don't enjoy being an 'also-ran' and would rather be an important part of a small organisation than a menial in a large one.

You should be lucky in love, and happy, provided you put in the effort to make a comfortable home for yourself and those close to you. It is likely that you will have a love of pleasure, sport, music and literature. Life brings you many rewards, most of them as a direct result of your own efforts, although you may be luckier than average and ready to make the best of any situation.

Moon in Virgo

You are endowed with good mental abilities and a keen receptive memory, but you are never ostentatious or pretentious. Naturally quite reserved, you still have many friends, especially of the opposite sex. Marital relationships must be discussed carefully and worked at so that they remain harmonious, as personal attachments can be a problem if you do not give them your full attention.

Talented and persevering, you possess artistic qualities and are a good homemaker. Earning your honours through genuine merit, you work long and hard towards your objectives but show little pride in your achievements. Many short journeys will be undertaken in your life.

Moon in Libra

With the Moon in Libra you are naturally popular and make friends easily. People like you, probably more than you realise, you bring fun to a party and are a natural diplomat. For all its good points, Libra is not the most stable of astrological signs and, as a result, your emotions can be a little unstable too. Therefore, although the Moon in Libra is said to be good for love and marriage, your Sun sign and Rising sign will have an important effect on your emotional and loving qualities.

You must remember to relate to others in your decision-making. Co-operation is crucial because Libra represents the 'balance' of life that can only be achieved through harmonious relationships. Conformity is not easy for you because Libra, an Air sign, likes its independence.

Moon in Scorpio

Some people might call you pushy. In fact, all you really want to do is to live life to the full and protect yourself and your family from the pressures of life. Take care to avoid giving the impression of being sarcastic or impulsive and use your energies wisely and constructively.

You have great courage and you invariably achieve your goals by force of personality and sheer effort. You are fond of mystery and are good at predicting the outcome of situations and events. Travel experiences can be beneficial to you.

You may experience problems if you do not take time to examine your motives in a relationship, and also if you allow jealousy, always a feature of Scorpio, to cloud your judgement.

Moon in Sagittarius

The Moon in Sagittarius helps to make you a generous individual with humanitarian qualities and a kind heart. Restlessness may be intrinsic as your mind is seldom still. Perhaps because of this, you have a need for change that could lead you to several major moves during your adult life. You are not afraid to stand your ground when you know your judgement is right, you speak directly and have good intuition.

At work you are quick, efficient and versatile and so you make an ideal employee. You need work to be intellectually demanding and do not enjoy tedious routines.

In relationships, you anger quickly if faced with stupidity or deception, though you are just as quick to forgive and forget. Emotionally, there are times when your heart rules your head.

Moon in Capricorn

The Moon in Capricorn makes you popular and likely to come into the public eye in some way. The watery Moon is not entirely comfortable in the Earth sign of Capricorn and this may lead to some difficulties in the early years of life. An initial lack of creative ability and indecision must be overcome before the true qualities of patience and perseverance inherent in Capricorn can show through.

You have good administrative ability and are a capable worker, and if you are careful you can accumulate wealth. But you must be cautious and take professional advice in partnerships, as you are open to deception. You may be interested in social or welfare work, which suit your organisational skills and sympathy for others.

Moon in Aquarius

The Moon in Aquarius makes you an active and agreeable person with a friendly, easy-going nature. Sympathetic to the needs of others, you flourish in a laid-back atmosphere. You are broad-minded, fair and open to suggestion, although sometimes you have an unconventional quality which others can find hard to understand.

You are interested in the strange and curious, and in old articles and places. You enjoy trips to these places and gain much from them. Political, scientific and educational work interests you and you might choose a career in science or technology.

Money-wise, you make gains through innovation and concentration and Lunar Aquarians often tackle more than one job at a time. In love you are kind and honest.

Moon in Pisces

You have a kind, sympathetic nature, somewhat retiring at times, but you always take account of others' feelings and help when you can.

Personal relationships may be problematic, but as life goes on you can learn from your experiences and develop a better understanding of yourself and the world around you.

You have a fondness for travel, appreciate beauty and harmony and hate disorder and strife. You may be fond of literature and would make a good writer or speaker yourself. You have a creative imagination and may come across as an incurable romantic. You have strong intuition, maybe bordering on a mediumistic quality, which sets you apart from the mass. You may not be rich in cash terms, but your personal gifts are worth more than gold.

ARIES IN LOVE

Discover how compatible in love you are with people from the same and other signs of the zodiac. Five stars equals a match made in heaven!

Aries meets Aries

This could be an all-or-nothing pairing. Both parties are from a dominant sign, so someone will have to be flexible in order to maintain personal harmony. Both know what they want out of life, and may have trouble overcoming any obstacles a relationship creates. This is a good physical pairing, with a chemistry that few other matches enjoy to the same level. Attitude is everything, but at least there is a mutual admiration that makes gazing at your partner like looking in the mirror. Star rating: ****

Aries meets Taurus

This is a match that has been known to work very well. Aries brings dynamism and ambition, while Taurus has the patience to see things through logically. Such complementary views work equally well in a relationship or in the office. There is mutual respect, but sometimes a lack of total understanding. The romantic needs of each are quite different, but both are still fulfilled. They can live easily in domestic harmony which is very important but, interestingly, Aries may be the loser in battles of will. Star rating: ***

Aries meets Gemini

Don't expect peace and harmony with this combination, although what comes along instead might make up for any disagreements. Gemini has a very fertile imagination, while Aries has the tenacity to make reality from fantasy. Combined, they have a sizzling relationship. There are times when both parties could explode with indignation and something has to give. But even if there are clashes, making them up will always be most enjoyable! Mutual financial success is likely in this match. Star rating: ****

Aries meets Cancer

A potentially one-sided pairing, it often appears that the Cancerian is brow-beaten by the far more dominant Arian. So much depends on the patience of the Cancerian individual, because if good psychology is present – who knows? But beware, Aries, you may find your partner too passive, and constantly having to take the lead can be wearing – even for you. A prolonged trial period would be advantageous, as the match could easily go either way. When it does work, though, this relationship is usually contented. Star rating: ***

Aries meets Leo

Stand by for action and make sure the house is sound-proof. Leo is a lofty idealist and there is always likely to be friction when two Fire signs meet. To compensate, there is much mutual admiration, together with a desire to please. Where there are shared incentives, the prognosis is good but it's important not to let little irritations blow up. Both signs want to have their own way and this is a sure cause of trouble. There might not be much patience here, but there is plenty of action. Star rating: *****

Aries meets Virgo

Neither of these signs really understands the other, and that could easily lead to a clash. Virgo is so pedantic, which will drive Aries up the wall, while Aries always wants to be moving on to the next objective, before Virgo is even settled with the last one. It will take time for these two to get to know each other, but this is a great business matching. If a personal relationship is seen in these terms then the prognosis can be good, but on the whole, this is not an inspiring match. Star rating: ***

Aries meets Libra

These signs are zodiac opposites which means a make-or-break situation. The match will either be a great success or a dismal failure. Why? Well Aries finds it difficult to understand the flighty Air-sign tendencies of Libra, whilst the natural balance of Libra contradicts the unorthodox Arian methods. Any flexibility will come from Libra, which may mean that things work out for a while, but Libra only has so much patience and it may eventually run out. In the end, Aries may be just too bossy for an independent but sensitive sign like Libra. Star rating: **

Aries meets Scorpio

There can be great affection here, even if the two zodiac signs are so very different. The common link is the planet Mars, which plays a part in both these natures. Although Aries is, outwardly, the most dominant, Scorpio people are among the most powerful to be found anywhere. This quiet determination is respected by Aries. Aries will satisfy the passionate side of Scorpio, particularly with instruction from Scorpio. There are mysteries here which will add spice to life. The few arguments that do occur are likely to be awe-inspiring. Star rating: ****

Aries meets Sagittarius

This can be one of the most favourable matches of them all. Both Aries and Sagittarius are Fire signs, which often leads to clashes of will, but this pair find a mutual understanding. Sagittarius helps Aries to develop a better sense of humour, while Aries teaches the Archer about consistency on the road to success. Some patience is called for on both sides, but these people have a natural liking for each other. Add this to growing love and you have a long-lasting combination that is hard to beat. Star rating: *****

Aries meets Capricorn

Capricorn works conscientiously to achieve its objectives and so can be the perfect companion for Aries. The Ram knows how to achieve but not how to consolidate, so the two signs have a great deal to offer one another practically. There may not be fireworks and it's sometimes doubtful how well they know each other, but it may not matter. Aries is outwardly hot but inwardly cool, whilst Capricorn can appear low key but be a furnace underneath. Such a pairing can gradually find contentment, though both parties may wonder how this is so. Star rating: ****

Aries meets Aquarius

Aquarius is an Air sign, and Air and Fire often work well together, but perhaps not in the case of Aries and Aquarius. The average Aquarian lives in what the Ram sees as a fantasy world, so without a sufficiently good meeting of minds, compromise may be lacking. Of course, almost anything is possible, and the dominant side of Aries could be trained by the devil-may-care attitude of Aquarius. There are meeting points but they are difficult to establish. However, given sufficient time and an open mind on both sides, a degree of happiness is possible. Star rating: **

Aries meets Pisces

Still waters run deep, and they don't come much deeper than Pisces. Although these signs share the same quadrant of the zodiac, they have little in common. Pisces is a dreamer, a romantic idealist with steady and spiritual goals. Aries needs to be on the move, and has very different ideals. It's hard to see how a relationship could develop because the outlook on life is so different but, with patience, especially from Aries, there is a chance that things might work out. Pisces needs incentive, and Aries may be the sign to offer it. Star rating: **

VENUS:
THE PLANET OF LOVE

If you look up at the sky around sunset or sunrise you will often see Venus in close attendance to the Sun. It is arguably one of the most beautiful sights of all and there is little wonder that historically it became associated with the goddess of love. But although Venus does play an important part in the way you view love and in the way others see you romantically, this is only one of the spheres of influence that it enjoys in your overall character.

Venus has a part to play in the more cultured side of your life and has much to do with your appreciation of art, literature, music and general creativity. Even the way you look is responsive to the part of the zodiac that Venus occupied at the start of your life, though this fact is also down to your Sun sign and Ascending sign. If, at the time you were born, Venus occupied one of the more gregarious zodiac signs, you will be more likely to wear your heart on your sleeve, as well as to be more attracted to entertainment, social gatherings and good company. If on the other hand Venus occupied a quiet zodiac sign at the time of your birth, you would tend to be more retiring and less willing to shine in public situations.

It's good to know what part the planet Venus plays in your life for it can have a great bearing on the way you appear to the rest of the world and since we all have to mix with others, you can learn to make the very best of what Venus has to offer you.

One of the great complications in the past has always been trying to establish exactly what zodiac position Venus enjoyed when you were born because the planet is notoriously difficult to track. However, we have solved that problem by creating a table that is exclusive to your Sun sign, which you will find on the following page.

Establishing your Venus sign could not be easier. Just look up the year of your birth on the following page and you will see a sign of the zodiac. This was the sign that Venus occupied in the period covered by your sign in that year. If Venus occupied more than one sign during the period, this is indicated by the date on which the sign changed, and the name of the new sign. For instance, if you were born in 1950, Venus was in Aquarius until the 7th April, after which time it was in Pisces. If you were born before 7th April your Venus sign is Aquarius, if you were born on or after 7th April, your Venus sign is Pisces. Once you have established the position of Venus at the time of your birth, you can then look in the pages which follow to see how this has a bearing on your life as a whole.

1920 PISCES / 14.4 ARIES
1921 TAURUS
1922 ARIES / 13.4 TAURUS
1923 AQUARIUS / 1.4 PISCES
1924 TAURUS / 6.4 GEMINI
1925 PISCES / 28.3 ARIES
1926 AQUARIUS / 6.4 PISCES
1927 ARIES / 24.3 TAURUS
1928 PISCES / 13.4 ARIES
1929 TAURUS / 20.4 ARIES
1930 ARIES / 13.4 TAURUS
1931 AQUARIUS / 31.3 PISCES
1932 TAURUS / 6.4 GEMINI
1933 PISCES / 27.3 ARIES
1934 AQUARIUS / 6.4 PISCES
1935 ARIES / 23.3 TAURUS
1936 PISCES / 13.4 ARIES
1937 TAURUS / 14.4 ARIES
1938 ARIES / 12.4 TAURUS
1939 AQUARIUS / 31.3 PISCES
1940 TAURUS / 5.4 GEMINI
1941 PISCES / 26.3 ARIES /
     20.4 TAURUS
1942 AQUARIUS / 7.4 PISCES
1943 ARIES / 23.3 TAURUS
1944 PISCES / 12.4 ARIES
1945 TAURUS / 8.4 ARIES
1946 ARIES / 12.4 TAURUS
1947 AQUARIUS / 30.3 PISCES
1948 TAURUS / 5.4 GEMINI
1949 PISCES / 25.3 ARIES /
     20.4 TAURUS
1950 AQUARIUS / 7.4 PISCES
1951 ARIES / 22.3 TAURUS
1952 PISCES / 12.4 ARIES
1953 TAURUS / 1.4 GEMINI
1954 ARIES / 11.4 TAURUS
1955 AQUARIUS / 30.3 PISCES
1956 TAURUS / 4.4 GEMINI
1957 PISCES / 25.3 ARIES /
     19.4 TAURUS
1958 AQUARIUS / 8.4 PISCES
1959 ARIES / 22.3 TAURUS
1960 PISCES / 11.4 ARIES
1961 ARIES
1962 ARIES / 11.4 TAURUS
1963 AQUARIUS / 29.3 PISCES
1964 TAURUS / 4.4 GEMINI
1965 PISCES / 24.3 ARIES /
     19.4 TAURUS
1966 AQUARIUS / 8.4 PISCES
1967 TAURUS / 20.4 GEMINI
1968 PISCES / 10.4 ARIES
1969 ARIES

1970 ARIES / 10.4 TAURUS
1971 AQUARIUS / 29.3 PISCES
1972 TAURUS / 3.4 GEMINI
1973 PISCES / 24.3 ARIES /
     18.4 TAURUS
1974 AQUARIUS / 8.4 PISCES
1975 TAURUS / 19.4 GEMINI
1976 PISCES / 10.4 ARIES
1977 ARIES
1978 ARIES / 10.4 TAURUS
1979 AQUARIUS / 28.3 PISCES
1980 TAURUS / 3.4 GEMINI
1981 PISCES / 23.3 ARIES /
     18.4 TAURUS
1982 AQUARIUS / 9.4 PISCES
1983 TAURUS / 19.4 GEMINI
1984 PISCES / 9.4 ARIES
1985 ARIES
1986 ARIES / 9.4 TAURUS
1987 AQUARIUS / 28.3 PISCES
1988 TAURUS / 2.4 GEMINI
1989 PISCES / 23.3 ARIES /
     17.4 TAURUS
1990 AQUARIUS / 9.4 PISCES
1991 TAURUS / 18.4 GEMINI
1992 PISCES / 9.4 ARIES
1993 ARIES
1994 ARIES / 9.4 TAURUS
1995 AQUARIUS / 27.3 PISCES
1996 TAURUS / 2.4 GEMINI
1997 PISCES / 22.3 ARIES /
     17.4 TAURUS
1998 AQUARIUS / 9.4 PISCES
1999 TAURUS / 18.4 GEMINI
2000 PISCES / 9.4 ARIES
2001 ARIES
2002 ARIES / 7.4 TAURUS
2003 AQUARIUS / 27.3 PISCES
2004 TAURUS / 1.4 GEMINI
2005 PISCES/22.3 ARIES
2006 AQUARIUS/7.4 PISCES
2007 TAURUS / 16.4 GEMINI
2008 PISCES / 9.4 ARIES
2009 ARIES
2010 ARIES / 7.4 TAURUS
2011 AQUARIUS / 27.3 PISCES
2012 TAURUS / 1.4 GEMINI
2013 PISCES / 22.3 ARIES
2014 AQUARIUS / 7.4 PISCES
2015 TAURUS / 16.4 GEMINI
2016 PISCES / 9.4 ARIES
2017 TAURUS / 1.4 GEMINI
2018 ARIES / 7.4 TAURUS

VENUS THROUGH THE ZODIAC SIGNS

Venus in Aries

Amongst other things, the position of Venus in Aries indicates a fondness for travel, music and all creative pursuits. Your nature tends to be affectionate and you would try not to create confusion or difficulty for others if it could be avoided. Many people with this planetary position have a great love of the theatre, and mental stimulation is of the greatest importance. Early romantic attachments are common with Venus in Aries, so it is very important to establish a genuine sense of romantic continuity. Early marriage is not recommended, especially if it is based on sympathy. You may give your heart a little too readily on occasions.

Venus in Taurus

You are capable of very deep feelings and your emotions tend to last for a very long time. This makes you a trusting partner and lover, whose constancy is second to none. In life you are precise and careful and always try to do things the right way. Although this means an ordered life, which you are comfortable with, it can also lead you to be rather too fussy for your own good. Despite your pleasant nature, you are very fixed in your opinions and quite able to speak your mind. Others are attracted to you and historical astrologers always quoted this position of Venus as being very fortunate in terms of marriage. However, if you find yourself involved in a failed relationship, it could take you a long time to trust again.

Venus in Gemini

As with all associations related to Gemini, you tend to be quite versatile, anxious for change and intelligent in your dealings with the world at large. You may gain money from more than one source but you are equally good at spending it. There is an inference here that you are a good communicator, via either the written or the spoken word, and you love to be in the company of interesting people. Always on the look-out for culture, you may also be very fond of music, and love to indulge the curious and cultured side of your nature. In romance you tend to have more than one relationship and could find yourself associated with someone who has previously been a friend or even a distant relative.

Venus in Cancer

You often stay close to home because you are very fond of family and enjoy many of your most treasured moments when you are with those you love. Being naturally sympathetic, you will always do anything you can to support those around you, even people you hardly know at all. This charitable side of your nature is your most noticeable trait and is one of the reasons why others are naturally so fond of you. Being receptive and in some cases even psychic, you can see through to the soul of most of those with whom you come into contact. You may not commence too many romantic attachments but when you do give your heart, it tends to be unconditionally.

Venus in Leo

It must become quickly obvious to almost anyone you meet that you are kind, sympathetic and yet determined enough to stand up for anyone or anything that is truly important to you. Bright and sunny, you warm the world with your natural enthusiasm and would rarely do anything to hurt those around you, or at least not intentionally. In romance you are ardent and sincere, though some may find your style just a little overpowering. Gains come through your contacts with other people and this could be especially true with regard to romance, for love and money often come hand in hand for those who were born with Venus in Leo. People claim to understand you, though you are more complex than you seem.

Venus in Virgo

Your nature could well be fairly quiet no matter what your Sun sign might be, though this fact often manifests itself as an inner peace and would not prevent you from being basically sociable. Some delays and even the odd disappointment in love cannot be ruled out with this planetary position, though it's a fact that you will usually find the happiness you look for in the end. Catapulting yourself into romantic entanglements that you know to be rather ill-advised is not sensible, and it would be better to wait before you committed yourself exclusively to any one person. It is the essence of your nature to serve the world at large and through doing so it is possible that you will attract money at some stage in your life.

Venus in Libra

Venus is very comfortable in Libra and bestows upon those people who have this planetary position a particular sort of kindness that is easy to recognise. This is a very good position for all sorts of friendships and also for romantic attachments that usually bring much joy into your life. Few individuals with Venus in Libra would avoid marriage and since you are capable of great depths of love, it is likely that you will find a contented personal life. You like to mix with people of integrity and intelligence but don't take kindly to scruffy surroundings or work that means getting your hands too dirty. Careful speculation, good business dealings and money through marriage all seem fairly likely.

Venus in Scorpio

You are quite open and tend to spend money quite freely, even on those occasions when you don't have very much. Although your intentions are always good, there are times when you get yourself in to the odd scrape and this can be particularly true when it comes to romance, which you may come to late or from a rather unexpected direction. Certainly you have the power to be happy and to make others contented on the way, but you find the odd stumbling block on your journey through life and it could seem that you have to work harder than those around you. As a result of this, you gain a much deeper understanding of the true value of personal happiness than many people ever do, and are likely to achieve true contentment in the end.

Venus in Sagittarius

You are lighthearted, cheerful and always able to see the funny side of any situation. These facts enhance your popularity, which is especially high with members of the opposite sex. You should never have to look too far to find romantic interest in your life, though it is just possible that you might be too willing to commit yourself before you are certain that the person in question is right for you. Part of the problem here extends to other areas of life too. The fact is that you like variety in everything and so can tire of situations that fail to offer it. All the same, if you choose wisely and learn to understand your restless side, then great happiness can be yours.

47

Venus in Capricorn

The most notable trait that comes from Venus in this position is that it makes you trustworthy and able to take on all sorts of responsibilities in life. People are instinctively fond of you and love you all the more because you are always ready to help those who are in any form of need. Social and business popularity can be yours and there is a magnetic quality to your nature that is particularly attractive in a romantic sense. Anyone who wants a partner for a lover, a spouse and a good friend too would almost certainly look in your direction. Constancy is the hallmark of your nature and unfaithfulness would go right against the grain. You might sometimes be a little too trusting.

Venus in Aquarius

This location of Venus offers a fondness for travel and a desire to try out something new at every possible opportunity. You are extremely easy to get along with and tend to have many friends from varied backgrounds, classes and inclinations. You like to live a distinct sort of life and gain a great deal from moving about, both in a career sense and with regard to your home. It is not out of the question that you could form a romantic attachment to someone who comes from far away or be attracted to a person of a distinctly artistic and original nature. What you cannot stand is jealousy, for you have friends of both sexes and would want to keep things that way.

Venus in Pisces

The first thing people tend to notice about you is your wonderful, warm smile. Being very charitable by nature you will do anything to help others, even if you don't know them well. Much of your life may be spent sorting out situations for other people, but it is very important to feel that you are living for yourself too. In the main, you remain cheerful, and tend to be quite attractive to members of the opposite sex. Where romantic attachments are concerned, you could be drawn to people who are significantly older or younger than yourself or to someone with a unique career or point of view. It might be best for you to avoid marrying whilst you are still very young.

ARIES:
2017 DIARY PAGES

October

2017

1 SUNDAY
Moon Age Day 11   Moon Sign Aquarius

You may find that you need to adapt if you want to get the very best out of life at the moment. For the last few days you have been under the influence of a few slightly awkward planetary influences and these could have left you feeling somewhat muddled. Today offers you the chance to think things through and to take action.

2 MONDAY
Moon Age Day 12   Moon Sign Aquarius

There could be a few troublesome domestic issues to be sorted out at the start of this week and that might lead to you getting behind in other matters. Exercise all the patience you can and simply do what seems necessary. You can catch up later and in any case it is a matter of priorities in the end.

3 TUESDAY
Moon Age Day 13   Moon Sign Pisces

Don't be bossy at home and allow family members to choose options for themselves. You don't mean to interfere, it's just your way, but others may not appreciate your seeming to know better than they do how to run their lives. If you listen and comment but avoid interference you can still have an input.

4 WEDNESDAY
Moon Age Day 14   Moon Sign Pisces

This could be one of the best times of the month for involving yourself in community issues and for getting to grips with a slight problem that has a bearing on just about everyone you know. You are very socially minded at the moment and the reforming tendencies of Aries show out strongly. You might even be quite political.

5 THURSDAY
Moon Age Day 15   Moon Sign Aries

Stand by for an explosion of possibilities and do everything you can to meet this very progressive period in a reactive way. The lunar high should bring better general luck, together with a fund of new incentives and plenty of energy to pursue them. All in all this could be the most influential day that you will encounter during October.

6 FRIDAY
Moon Age Day 16   Moon Sign Aries

This is the best time of the month to be running ahead of the pack. So quick are your thought processes that it is unlikely many people will be able to keep up with you. The new incentives continue and at the same time you have what it takes to sweep someone right off their feet. New romance is possible for some.

7 SATURDAY
Moon Age Day 17   Moon Sign Taurus

Don't allow the views of others to influence your judgements to such an extent that you fail to address issues yourself. Aries might be just a little lazy at the moment and for that reason alone it will be easier to simply go with the flow. Force yourself to think about matters yourself and take whatever actions your mind suggests.

8 SUNDAY
Moon Age Day 18   Moon Sign Taurus

You need to keep moving and to follow up all possibilities as and when they arise. There won't be too much time to spend with loved ones but even a few words of reassurance might be all it takes to keep things sweet at home. Meanwhile you will be going wherever the action is and should stay well in charge of your own destiny.

9 MONDAY
Moon Age Day 19   Moon Sign Taurus

You enjoy a good balance of give and take right now and should find certain individuals to be far more giving than might have been the case only a few days ago. With plenty of determination you won't be easily beaten but there might be one particular issue that despite all your efforts should now be reluctantly abandoned.

10 TUESDAY
Moon Age Day 20   Moon Sign Gemini

Organisational issues take up a good deal of your time at the moment. This could be related to work but is just as likely to be concerned with social issues and your need to ring the changes in terms of out-of-work interests. Keep in touch with friends who are at a distance and maybe arrange a long journey to be taken next year.

11 WEDNESDAY
Moon Age Day 21   Moon Sign Gemini

Don't allow yourself to be manipulated by others but instead look at all situations yourself and react according to your own conscience. Aries is a natural leader and not a follower, which is why in the end you may bring others round to your own point of view. It's a fine line, though, because bullying certainly won't work at present.

12 THURSDAY
Moon Age Day 22   Moon Sign Cancer

Life can be somewhat trying in some ways and yet very positive in others – it's simply a matter of choosing your path carefully for the moment. Although you may be on the receiving end of many social invitations, you may now be in the mood to stay close to home and the incentives to move around are not strong.

13 FRIDAY
Moon Age Day 23   Moon Sign Cancer

It may not be at all easy to stay on top of things and you have to ask yourself whether it is even necessary in some cases. There might be certain issues that would be best left to their own devices, whilst you concentrate on matters that are self-evidently important. In any case your capabilities are going to be much improved later.

14 SATURDAY
Moon Age Day 24   Moon Sign Leo

A restless streak starts to become evident and ordinary, everyday tasks could be something you will run a mile to avoid. You need a change of scenery and even if you only manage to get an hour or two in your local park it could be enough to make you feel entirely different. Learn to delegate and let others do some of the work.

15 SUNDAY
Moon Age Day 25   Moon Sign Leo

Home and family seem to remain the most important consideration for you this Sunday and although friends might be urging you to do different things, many Arians will be quite happy to stay around the homestead for the moment. New incentives come along tomorrow but for the moment find a chair and sit in it.

16 MONDAY
Moon Age Day 26   Moon Sign Virgo

You should bring out your intellectual gifts now and use them for all you are worth. Half way between intuitive and inspirational you can make almost anything go your way. You will also thrive on the fact that there are several tasks to be taken on at the same time and you won't easily be thwarted by the odd setback.

17 TUESDAY
Moon Age Day 27   Moon Sign Virgo

Positive influences surround social encounters and you will be happiest when you are dealing with a number of different groups or organisations. That way when you tire of one thing you can move on to another. There is more than a little ingenuity about you at present and that makes you wonderful to have around when a minor panic sets in.

18 WEDNESDAY
Moon Age Day 28   Moon Sign Libra

Communication issues could run into difficulty if you don't keep on top of them. The basic reason is that others will misunderstand what you are trying to tell them and it is therefore very important that you double-check that messages are coming across as you intend. This is more likely to be an issue at work than in social settings.

19 THURSDAY
Moon Age Day 29   Moon Sign Libra

It will probably become obvious today why things are breaking down a little. For this you can thank the lunar low, which is inclined to make you rather muddled in your thinking and actions. There is a funny side to this, however, because others find you charming and will be more than happy to smile kindly on your eccentricities.

20 FRIDAY
Moon Age Day 0   Moon Sign Libra

This is a time to get ahead by jumping the queue. Such is your charm that nobody will worry too much that you are not waiting around to be asked, and in any case this is not the way Aries acts when working at its best. In addition to having a silver tongue at present you also exhibit tremendous intuition, a gift without parallel.

21 SATURDAY
Moon Age Day 1   Moon Sign Scorpio

You demonstrate a tremendous talent for persuasion, even in situations that would have colleagues or friends baffled. For some reason people actively want to follow your lead and since they recognise that 'winner' is written through you like a stick of rock, they may well be willing to invest in you.

22 SUNDAY
Moon Age Day 2   Moon Sign Scorpio

Mental restlessness at this time could, and indeed should, incline you to abandon traditional ways of getting things done in favour of seeking out new ideas or situations. It's all about stimulation whilst present trends last and you need to feel that payback is due for all the effort you have put into life. Others find you exotic and intriguing.

23 MONDAY
Moon Age Day 3   Moon Sign Sagittarius

This might turn out to be the best time of the month to be the centre of attention. People are pleased to have you around and it will be easy for you to find the right words to impress just about anyone. You will be especially good at influencing superiors and may find yourself on the receiving end of an intriguing offer.

24 TUESDAY
Moon Age Day 4   Moon Sign Sagittarius

You may have to look again at a recent project at work and this time bring a little more ingenuity to bear on it than you did before. In affairs of the heart you could discover that normal responses won't work and that you will have to be slightly more ingenious in your approach. Pay attention to all the small details of life.

25 WEDNESDAY   *Moon Age Day 5   Moon Sign Sagittarius*

If you remain fairly committed to home and family this is mainly because of what is happening to those you love. There are new incentives for younger people and maybe a positive reversal in the health of someone who has been out of sorts for a while. A little gossip may be especially appealing to you today.

26 THURSDAY   *Moon Age Day 6   Moon Sign Capricorn*

Your mind is working fast and you might tend to express yourself in a hurried manner. No sooner do you arrive somewhere than you are on the move again and your actions might make those around you slightly dizzy. A link with the past could turn out to be quite meaningful and may cause you to think deeply.

27 FRIDAY   *Moon Age Day 7   Moon Sign Capricorn*

Family life is certain to bring out the best in you under present planetary trends. Home is the place where you bring extended entertainment and you may be planning already for an 'at home' sort of weekend to come. As the days get colder your fireside seems more welcoming but your social instincts remain strong.

28 SATURDAY   *Moon Age Day 8   Moon Sign Aquarius*

This is a marvellous time to get out into the social world – or even more likely to attract it to your own door. You do need to make new contacts and there are any number of fascinating possibilities in the pipeline. The week ahead may have positive changes in store so prepare for them now if you can.

29 SUNDAY   *Moon Age Day 9   Moon Sign Aquarius*

Planetary movements right now make you intellectually inspirational and very exciting. Many of the gains and benefits that arrive now come like a bolt from the blue and it is important to stand ready to make your move at almost any time. When you are away from work you now find it easier to relax and to make the most of family moments.

30 MONDAY
Moon Age Day 10   Moon Sign Pisces

Expect some kind of high point as far as your general plans are concerned and don't be afraid to use every skill in your armoury to get where you want to be. If this means gently nudging someone else out of the way then so be it. Worry about helping them along once you are where you rightfully belong. You can't afford to be too sensitive today.

31 TUESDAY
Moon Age Day 11   Moon Sign Pisces

A domestic matter could prove tiresome in some way, probably mainly because there is so much you want to do out there in the wider world. Feelings may be coming to the surface and that means serious talks – something that you don't really want at the moment. Nevertheless you should take the time out to try to understand.

November

1 WEDNESDAY   *Moon Age Day 12   Moon Sign Pisces*

Your present ability to fully enjoy life is likely to prove infectious to others and there isn't much doubt that you will be spreading your goodwill far and wide today. Aries comes across at its sunny and generous best, which means everyone loves you. This is certainly a very positive way to approach the lunar high tomorrow.

2 THURSDAY   *Moon Age Day 13   Moon Sign Aries*

This is likely to be one of the best days of the month for getting what you want and for being able to keep everyone else happy on the way. You won't be easily dissuaded from any course of action you want to take but since you also have what it takes to talk others round to your particular point of view all should be well.

3 FRIDAY   *Moon Age Day 14   Moon Sign Aries*

Things continue to look very good as far as your life is concerned and you should be registering a whole host of reasons why you can smile most of the time. Past successes become present ones, whilst you are also able to project yourself with great enthusiasm into situations that appear out of the blue. Life is on your side now.

4 SATURDAY   *Moon Age Day 15   Moon Sign Taurus*

Plenty of enjoyable things seem to be happening as far as your social life is concerned though personal attachments probably need more attention on your part and you could do worse than deliberately planning to sweep your partner or sweetheart off their feet in some way. Every little favour you do others today will be more than welcome.

5 SUNDAY
Moon Age Day 16   Moon Sign Taurus

Pleasure and enjoyment are high on your agenda now and you won't want to be so busy with practical issues that you fail to register the good times that are on offer. On the contrary you now have what it takes to bring a great deal of joy to even the most mundane tasks and on the way you are about as entertaining as you can be.

6 MONDAY
Moon Age Day 17   Moon Sign Gemini

Though you are quite able to bring out the best in others in social situations right now, you may be having slightly less success making them keep their heads down at work. Part of the reason lies in the fact that you are so happy-go-lucky yourself at present. In addition there are trends around indicating this to be a fairly positive time financially.

7 TUESDAY
Moon Age Day 18   Moon Sign Gemini

A trip into the past might seem to be especially rewarding at the moment and for once this could genuinely turn out to be the case for Aries. This is not because you are becoming especially nostalgic but rather because you are learning lessons as a result of happenings now long gone. It is upon such lessons that wisdom is founded.

8 WEDNESDAY
Moon Age Day 19   Moon Sign Cancer

You are still pushing forward very progressively but should heed a few words of warning with regard to finances at the moment. You are not immune to a little bad luck when it comes to almost any sort of speculation and you could lose money if you fail to think before you act. In almost every other respect, life should remain positive and happy.

9 THURSDAY
Moon Age Day 20   Moon Sign Cancer

Most aspects of life can be aided now not by what you know but by who you know. Keep your eyes open for individuals who are in a position to help you out with an idea or a long-term plan for the future. There ought to be time enough today to discuss such matters and to enlist the support of individuals you like and respect.

10 FRIDAY
Moon Age Day 21   Moon Sign Leo

You are hardly likely to be waylaid by domestic chores or considerations at the moment, simply because you are so busy with the practical necessities of life. Don't be too quick to take offence when a colleague or friend seems to be critical. What they are saying is probably for your own good – even if that seems doubtful.

11 SATURDAY
Moon Age Day 22   Moon Sign Leo

A strong desire for social situations is noteworthy this weekend and whether or not you work at the weekend your mind is likely to be given over to pleasure at some stage. You will be delighted if you have a reason to paint the town red, but if not you should be able to invent one if you think hard enough.

12 SUNDAY
Moon Age Day 23   Moon Sign Virgo

You find yourself in some very enjoyable company today and will relish the cut and thrust of a busy and enjoyable time. Not everyone will want to join in the fun and games and it may be necessary to ask a few pertinent questions if someone close to you is especially quiet. Try to draw them out and discover what is wrong.

13 MONDAY
Moon Age Day 24   Moon Sign Virgo

The necessities of life might appear to be limiting your personal freedom today but that may be only because you are holding on to issues that you could reasonably abandon right now. A fresh approach to some aspects of your life is probably necessary, together with the input of your partner or some very close friends.

14 TUESDAY
Moon Age Day 25   Moon Sign Libra

The lunar low is inclined to take the wind out of your sails now but probably not as much as would sometimes be the case. You can use the quieter tendencies that today brings in order to refuel your tanks and also for thinking ahead of yourself. Not everyone is on your side at the moment but when it matters they will be.

15 WEDNESDAY   *Moon Age Day 26   Moon Sign Libra*

Keep life as simple as possible for the moment and don't complicate issues more than strictly necessary. An uncluttered day will mean that you have more time to think up future strategies. Take time to register the fact that colleagues and friends alike are now proving to be especially helpful and make a note to return the favours later.

16 THURSDAY   *Moon Age Day 27   Moon Sign Libra*

This is an especially good time to be working in groups or with individuals you really like. Colleagues might be demanding but they ask as much of themselves as they will of you and that makes all the difference. You can't do enough at the moment for someone you really like and that could be just about everyone.

17 FRIDAY   *Moon Age Day 28   Moon Sign Scorpio*

The lunar low has passed and this is a time when you can happily see yourself in the limelight and enjoy all the accolades that are coming your way. Most of what you are doing involves subjects you understand only too well, which is why you maintain so much confidence. Only rarely will you come unstuck in conversations and these moments will be funny.

18 SATURDAY   *Moon Age Day 0   Moon Sign Scorpio*

You need to take plenty of time to make up your mind about personal matters and probably should not be taking any precipitous decisions for the moment. Let things ride and allow yourself more room to look at the broader possibilities of life. Sooner or later you will have to make choices but certainly not today.

19 SUNDAY   *Moon Age Day 1   Moon Sign Sagittarius*

Domestic matters should be turning out very much in the way you would wish, but there could be something at the back of your mind that niggles away. Perhaps you have worries about a relative or you could think that you have inadvertently upset someone? Either way the chances are that you are overplaying the situation.

20 MONDAY
Moon Age Day 2   Moon Sign Sagittarius

A slightly nostalgic mood could prevail today and it is likely that you would relish a less demanding role for a few hours. Wallowing in the past is not usually your thing but for once it is likely to bring out the best in you. There are also lessons to be learned and some laughter over the things you did once upon a time.

21 TUESDAY
Moon Age Day 3   Moon Sign Sagittarius

Positive highlights appear within social and leisure interests. You should discover that your popularity is at a peak and your impressive personality is a definite boon. At work you will be more than capable and can show colleagues and superiors alike how efficient the zodiac sign of Aries can be. All attention is focused on your actions.

22 WEDNESDAY
Moon Age Day 4   Moon Sign Capricorn

Don't rush ahead too much with practical decisions just now. There are many options around and you will want to look at all of them before you set to a fixed course of action. This runs contrary to the usual Aries way of proceeding because you are generally inclined to act or react extremely quickly.

23 THURSDAY
Moon Age Day 5   Moon Sign Capricorn

Your forte right now is to make a comfortable home environment and to enjoy the quieter and less strenuous possibilities that come along during the winter months. Not that you enjoy this time of year very much. Aries is a creature of the spring and any possibility to feel the warmth of the sun somewhere else should be seriously considered.

24 FRIDAY
Moon Age Day 6   Moon Sign Aquarius

What a great day this would be for romance and for showing your partner just how important they are to you. If you are between relationships at the moment now is one of the best times to concentrate your efforts and to impress someone who could become quite special. Take care not to indulge too much with food and drink.

25 SATURDAY   *Moon Age Day 7   Moon Sign Aquarius*

Take full advantage of emotional links with friends and family and also spend some time today planning with others how the Christmas period is going to be handled. Someone extremely close to you could unintentionally be a great help and you make the most of all little opportunities to prove how loyal you are.

26 SUNDAY   *Moon Age Day 8   Moon Sign Aquarius*

A sense of optimism and a thirst for new ideas permeates practically everything you are doing at this stage of the month. You love being pleasant to others and what you get in return is not only affection but a great deal of practical help too. There are so many people queuing up at the moment to do you favours it could be embarrassing.

27 MONDAY   *Moon Age Day 9   Moon Sign Pisces*

Home is where you would probably prefer to be today but instead you are thrust out into an unsuspecting world. All sorts of family matters benefit from your wisdom and common sense when you are able to curl up by your own fireside, whereas more practical matters may seem to be awkward and difficult today.

28 TUESDAY   *Moon Age Day 10   Moon Sign Pisces*

Daily affairs should be more enjoyable now due to pleasant domestic influences and you should discover that loved ones have your best interests at heart. All of this makes for a pleasant sort of Tuesday but one that also demands a certain amount of effort on your part. What a great day this would be for a trip to town. Christmas shopping calls!

29 WEDNESDAY   *Moon Age Day 11   Moon Sign Aries*

Now you get the chance to take the initiative and to demonstrate how good your ideas really are. The lunar high coincides with the middle of a busy week and it is in practical and professional matters that you tend to excel. Good fortune is on your side and so you can afford to push your luck a lot more than you usually might.

30 THURSDAY
Moon Age Day 12   Moon Sign Aries

Even failure could be turned into sparkling success right now, though you need to focus all your attention in specific directions if you are to really show your worth. There is great warmth around at the moment, even though the weather is likely to be anything but warm. Your cheery smile will light up everyone's world.

December

2017

1 FRIDAY
Moon Age Day 13   Moon Sign Taurus

Your love life and romantic matters generally should be a definite high spot around now, but if this is not the case it may be that you are failing to put in sufficient effort. Also, in the everyday world, present planetary trends indicate that this would be just about the best time for getting others to back your ideas.

2 SATURDAY
Moon Age Day 14   Moon Sign Taurus

When it comes to getting on with things you may find that it can work wonders to work as a pair. You are inclined to want to group together with like-minded individuals and certainly won't be short of help when you need it the most. Your naturally warm and happy disposition begins to show through.

3 SUNDAY
☿ *Moon Age Day 15   Moon Sign Gemini*

Get out and about today – it doesn't really matter where because it's the contacts you meet along the way that are important. You may want to avoid humdrum and everyday jobs, and either leave them to others or ignore them altogether. Life itself is your best teacher at present, as you are about to discover.

4 MONDAY
☿ *Moon Age Day 16   Moon Sign Gemini*

It is very important for you to spare more than a passing thought for the feelings and sensibilities of your partner today. If you are not involved in one specific relationship at present the trends are still around but instead they may have a bearing on close family ties. Take time out to work out why others are behaving in the way they are.

5 TUESDAY ☿ *Moon Age Day 17   Moon Sign Cancer*

This heralds the start of a period of enjoyment and emotional fulfilment, though once again it is important that you take note of what is happening around you if you want to get the very best from these trends. One thing is more or less certain – you can get more of your own way now without having to work too hard to do so.

6 WEDNESDAY ☿ *Moon Age Day 18   Moon Sign Cancer*

You are now likely to be entering a harmonious phase in personal and romantic attachments. Working together as one of a pair is going to seem quite natural to you and even where there has been disagreement and disharmony, peace is now likely to prevail. Give some extra thought to last minute details.

7 THURSDAY ☿ *Moon Age Day 19   Moon Sign Leo*

In terms of your financial life there is now a good chance you will have to alter your plans in some way. Maybe an investment you made will cease to bring the return you would wish or it could be that you are simply re-thinking your overall strategies. There is time today to consider such matters, and incentives to do so.

8 FRIDAY ☿ *Moon Age Day 20   Moon Sign Leo*

Your personal ego is very strong at the moment and you could so easily lose your temper if others cross you about issues that you see as being your own. Before you fly off the handle, remember the time of year and just let things flow over you. Routines might seem to be quite inviting at some stage in today's proceedings.

9 SATURDAY ☿ *Moon Age Day 21   Moon Sign Virgo*

It shouldn't be difficult to get yourself into the limelight this weekend and the approach of the festive season sweeps you up in all sorts of fun activities. Whether you are with friends, colleagues or your partner, now is the time to shake free from the bonds of convention and to do something extraordinary.

10 SUNDAY ☿ *Moon Age Day 22   Moon Sign Virgo*

You are likely to delight in romantic relationships and this is a perfect day for checking out the most exciting social events and for signing yourself up to them. You certainly intend to be noticed and won't let any opportunity pass you by. The only slight downside is that there could be some fairly awkward types about.

11 MONDAY ☿ *Moon Age Day 23   Moon Sign Virgo*

Your plans and objectives could be advanced by some brand new information that comes your way. In a particularly chatty mood right now, you will also be keen to listen to what others have to say. Being nosey can sometimes work out to your advantage but it doesn't do anything for that Fire-sign Aries persona.

12 TUESDAY ☿ *Moon Age Day 24   Moon Sign Libra*

The lunar low this time around is likely to make you rather more circumspect and maybe inclined to look back, rather than projecting your ideas into the future. It won't be too much of a struggle to force yourself to take time out to do whatever takes your fancy. In any case trying too hard today and tomorrow simply won't work.

13 WEDNESDAY ☿ *Moon Age Day 25   Moon Sign Libra*

Energy and enthusiasm remains in generally short supply for now and the best way you can enjoy today is to let others do most of the work whilst you sit back and supervise. Aries can be quite good at delegation and in any case the time is probably right to let others, and especially younger people, have their moment.

14 THURSDAY ☿ *Moon Age Day 26   Moon Sign Scorpio*

You have a strong desire to make your domestic surroundings just as comfortable as can be. Loved ones have a great deal to contribute and you shouldn't belittle their contributions, even accidentally. Think before you speak and make sure to heap special praise on people who genuinely have done well of late.

15 FRIDAY
☿ *Moon Age Day 27   Moon Sign Scorpio*

Your desire for romance should be more than fulfilled today. This trend renews and invigorates relationships and makes it possible for you to whisper those special words that mean so much to your partner. Those Arians who don't have someone special in their lives at present should look towards new possibilities.

16 SATURDAY
☿ *Moon Age Day 28   Moon Sign Scorpio*

Minor plans start to bear real fruit and the result could be gains you hadn't really expected. For one thing you could suddenly find yourself slightly better off, though you won't have any problem spending money either. Your main concern today will be perceptive planning for the way ahead.

17 SUNDAY
☿ *Moon Age Day 29   Moon Sign Sagittarius*

Look out for a period of advancement. It could be that you are being looked upon favourably at work or that you receive an unexpected bonus. Whatever happens today you tend to take things in your stride and react very quickly to changing circumstances. People from the past might also reappear today.

18 MONDAY
☿ *Moon Age Day 0   Moon Sign Sagittarius*

Focus your sights on love and romance. This is where the joy resides under present trends and right now comes a certain warmth that isn't possible at other times of year. Plans should be well laid for Christmas but as usual you will want to change some of them, so be aware that this could upset family members.

19 TUESDAY
☿ *Moon Age Day 1   Moon Sign Capricorn*

With a king-sized ego at the moment this is the time to strike out on your own and to make it plain to an unsuspecting world that you really are a typical Aries. You are likely to be energetic and may find the slight impositions brought about by the special needs of December getting in your way. Never mind, you will be festive later.

20 WEDNESDAY ☿ Moon Age Day 2   Moon Sign Capricorn

Today you can expect an increase in all pleasurable endeavours. It's amazing where all your present energy is coming from and you should be enjoying life to the full. New and better possibilities at work might come about as a result of someone else's slightly bad luck but you can't blame yourself for that eventuality.

21 THURSDAY ☿ Moon Age Day 3   Moon Sign Capricorn

Weigh up the balance between family commitments and the need to do something for yourself. If you are certain you have fulfilled your obligations then you can afford to be slightly selfish today – although others probably won't see it in that way. Don't be too influenced by your perception of the expectations of others.

22 FRIDAY ☿ Moon Age Day 4   Moon Sign Aquarius

You now enjoy social gatherings and also the chance to be part of a team – though there is no doubt that you still adopt a fairly dominant role. Nobody will be surprised about this because it is, after all, what is expected from Aries. At the same time you are honourable and able to admit when you are wrong.

23 SATURDAY Moon Age Day 5   Moon Sign Aquarius

A practical plan ought to be coming together very nicely and you won't have to look too far to find any answers you require. Friends and colleagues alike should prove to be especially helpful and it is possible that you can put something important to bed ahead of the prolonged period of festivities that lie ahead of you.

24 SUNDAY Moon Age Day 6   Moon Sign Pisces

Although you may not be able to express yourself quite so well today when in great gatherings of people, the same will not be true in an intimate sense. You know exactly the right words to say in order to make someone feel really good and if you are specifically looking at the possibility of making a romantic conquest do it today.

25 MONDAY
Moon Age Day 7   Moon Sign Pisces

Special attachments put the biggest smile on your face for Christmas Day and everything comes together in a planetary sense to offer you the best of times. Not everyone will enjoy themselves, of course, but that's Christmas. Leave the Scrooges and the miseries alone and concentrate on the fun types.

26 TUESDAY
Moon Age Day 8   Moon Sign Pisces

Widening your horizons as much as possible seems to be your thing for today. You will probably get round to looking at all those presents and there could have been something in your stocking that turns out to be especially significant. You may want to take a journey today but don't undertake it on your own.

27 WEDNESDAY
Moon Age Day 9   Moon Sign Aries

Lady Luck is about to pay you a visit, even if you don't realise it until sometime further down the line. Make this a day to remember by taking command of situations and by refusing to take no for an answer when you feel a yes in your soul. Aries is now aspiring, noble, courageous and determined. Wow! What a person you can be.

28 THURSDAY
Moon Age Day 10   Moon Sign Aries

Major endeavours and undertakings go better when you are involved and others are almost certain to realise it. This is not a time during which you will have to fight to be heard. On the contrary, people will be seeking you out because they know you always take a very positive attitude to life. Show your romantic side today.

29 FRIDAY
Moon Age Day 11   Moon Sign Taurus

Today finds you doing well in social gatherings and being the life and soul of family parties. Even on those occasions when you have to be pleasant to people you don't especially care for you will do better than you expect and the love you shower in the direction of family members is well received and returned.

30 SATURDAY   *Moon Age Day 12   Moon Sign Taurus*

Along comes a potential high spot for those of you who are working over the Christmas holidays. If you toil away in the retail trade you will be especially busy at the moment but that won't worry you with your current high energy levels. Arians who can relax today probably won't do so at all. There are bargains to be had, so get off to the shops and bag a few.

31 SUNDAY   *Moon Age Day 13   Moon Sign Gemini*

For New Year's Eve you have what it takes to adopt any kind of prominent role and will continue to be at the centre of whatever is taking place in your vicinity. This is Aries at its best and you won't be stuck for ideas, even when others are finding the going difficult. If there is any race to be won, Aries can cross the line first.

ARIES:
2018 DIARY PAGES

ARIES:
YOUR YEAR IN BRIEF

As the year begins, the planets suggest that people with the zodiac sign of Aries will be acting cautiously. This is quite unusual for your sign, but it is sensible under prevailing circumstances. The fact that you are exercising a little self-discipline and organising yourself rather more than usual increases your chances of ultimate success. The end of February looks likely to bring some quite startling surprises.

The months of March and April begin to look fairly progressive, even if you find yourself a little down in the dumps as you struggle through the early spring weather. The temperature may not be warm but love can certainly be so and these could be two of the best months of the year for romance. As the weeks advance you will notice that something begins to awaken inside you and energy returns. Make the most of new social opportunities in late April.

May and June usher in the summer, a time of year that is likely to be a favourite for you. The better weather and longer days offer you more freedom and a new sense of purpose. On top form and at your most popular, June, in particular, may see you making some startling progress. Conversations can prove to be especially informative and potentially rewarding.

The arrival of midsummer is the best time of all for most Arians. July and August is the time when you will be travelling the most and when you are looking around at the world and seeing the variety of opportunities that surround you. Your attention to detail isn't always what it might be and there may be times when you have to do the same thing over again but in the main you are positive, cheerful and ambitious. New love is possible in August.

As the autumn winds start to blow, the arrival of September might find you a little more reserved and slightly less inclined to push yourself forward than before, although usually only for a day or two at a time. General trends in the later stages of the year incline you to be cheerful, enterprising and kind. October could be luckier than expected and might bring news of some foreign travel for next year. Keep a sense of proportion regarding the actions of younger people.

At the close of the year, November and December have plenty to offer in terms of personal happiness and you should be keen to make a great deal more of Christmas this time around than would often be the case. November sees you anxious to make progress at work, whilst December reverberates with personal possibilities and should offer more in the way of romance. The very end of the year offers new opportunities of a distinctly financial nature.

January 2018

1 MONDAY
Moon Age Day 14   Moon Sign Gemini

The first day of the year is likely to see you feeling mentally sharp and focused. However, bear in mind that it is important not to rush things because you will ultimately make much better progress if you take your time. You can also expect not to have much patience with or incentive for pointless routines around now.

2 TUESDAY
Moon Age Day 15   Moon Sign Cancer

You certainly have an easy-going nature at this stage of January and this could win you quite a lot of friends. Be certain of your ground before you suggest any major changes that could have a bearing on your professional life. It is possible to back yourself into a corner that wouldn't normally be of your own choosing.

3 WEDNESDAY
Moon Age Day 16   Moon Sign Cancer

Although you might appear nervous in some situations, your usual Arian confidence will rise to the fore. In any sort of sporting activity you are now inclined to go for gold and you won't allow people to stand in your way regarding any issue about which you have definitely made up your mind.

4 THURSDAY
Moon Age Day 17   Moon Sign Leo

This should be a highly satisfactory and a very productive time for you, with plenty of trends about that help you in a financial and a practical sense. Although you are usually happy in your attitude to life, now you are sunnier than ever. This mood could see you make new friends, one or two of whom could prove to be particularly useful soon.

5 FRIDAY
Moon Age Day 18   Moon Sign Leo

You may be feeling especially emotional, and your ego is dominant, although that's nothing new for Aries. But despite your Fire-sign nature you are unlikely to lord it over others. With a chance to make a favourable romantic impression, young or young-at-heart Arians are especially well off at this stage of the week.

6 SATURDAY
Moon Age Day 19   Moon Sign Virgo

Expect some conflict at the moment between yourself and a loved one. Although there might be very little you can do to address this situation at present, at least thinking about it should help. This might not be the most rewarding Saturday you will ever experience but it does have good social possibilities.

7 SUNDAY
Moon Age Day 20   Moon Sign Virgo

Most of your plans can now proceed in an orderly and disciplined manner. Of course you cannot rely on the support of everyone you know, but anyone who won't play ball should not create a hindrance. The more boring the job you take on today, the better you are likely to deal with it. Surprise surprise!

8 MONDAY
Moon Age Day 21   Moon Sign Libra

A sudden brake is put on your activities and progress as the monthly lunar low comes along. There is nothing else for it but to watch and wait for a while. Launching any new enterprise is not to be considered for today or tomorrow. Consolidate your position and be willing to bide your time.

9 TUESDAY
Moon Age Day 22   Moon Sign Libra

There really is no point in taking on anything you know is going to lead to a rough ride today, even if it means someone is disappointed. Make your excuses if necessary and stick by your instincts. It isn't long until tomorrow, by which time your reserve will disappear and your optimism will rise to full strength.

10 WEDNESDAY   *Moon Age Day 23   Moon Sign Scorpio*

You should be able to get the best from both work and practical matters at this time. Don't be reluctant to put your point of view forward with confidence, but avoid crossing swords with people you know to be at least your intellectual equals. Pointless arguments will only prove a waste of everyone's time.

11 THURSDAY   *Moon Age Day 24   Moon Sign Scorpio*

Though you may now feel less in control of your own affairs than is usual for people born under the sign of Aries, it is unlikely that this realisation will cause any undue stress. Give yourself to the moment and enjoy the cut and thrust of the solid relationship trends that are building at this time. Planning for tomorrow may be necessary.

12 FRIDAY   *Moon Age Day 25   Moon Sign Scorpio*

Prepare for the fact that a personal matter might leave you feeling confused. You might need to ask the advice of someone you trust but you will not want to allow the recent pace of your progress to be slowed. Coming to terms with the past should be easy enough if you remain philosophical.

13 SATURDAY   *Moon Age Day 26   Moon Sign Sagittarius*

Sometimes unforeseen opportunities arise without any input from you. If something takes you by surprise today, don't hold back but use your motivational skills to move forward, even if you do encounter some obstacles along the way. Few will match your powers of persuasion now.

14 SUNDAY   *Moon Age Day 27   Moon Sign Sagittarius*

You really do need to keep your eye on the ball right now. There is time for contemplation this Sunday, and it may also be helpful to seek sound advice from people who are in the know. Aspects of the past could prove to be important and in themselves offer invaluable advice for the future.

15 MONDAY   *Moon Age Day 28   Moon Sign Capricorn*

Try to look at life from a different point of view this week but be a realist – refuse to take an over optimistic view of anything. Stay away from any unnecessary arguments and look for peaceful solutions to all potential problems if at all possible. Most important of all, get out and about.

16 TUESDAY   *Moon Age Day 0   Moon Sign Capricorn*

Keep a tight hold on your purse strings for the moment because the planet Mars is doing you no real favours, except warning you against pushing the boat out too much and too frequently. Applying yourself isn't difficult and you tend to be looking more at the medium and long-term future than at today.

17 WEDNESDAY   *Moon Age Day 1   Moon Sign Capricorn*

Someone could be trying to set you up and although this might not necessarily prove to be an unpleasant experience, you should be prepared for it all the same. It makes a change when someone manages to fool you or play some sort of joke on you; as a rule it's the other way round. It may be difficult to conform to expectations today.

18 THURSDAY   *Moon Age Day 2   Moon Sign Aquarius*

If you are not in too much of a hurry today you may find you get on far better than if you rush your fences. Watch and wait, because that's the way to be in the best possible position to benefit from some of the opportunities that stand around you. In speech you will be quick and decisive, no matter what company you are in.

19 FRIDAY   *Moon Age Day 3   Moon Sign Aquarius*

There may now be some material gains around that you didn't expect to be coming your way. It's all a matter of receiving rewards as a result of past efforts, rather than thanks to anything you are doing right now. Your concern for the underdog is strong and you will be doing a great deal today to support and help your friends.

20 SATURDAY
Moon Age Day 4   Moon Sign Pisces

New initiatives at work are the name of the game for you today and you apply yourself very positively to anything you decide to take on. It is possible that you will be working slightly too hard on occasions but you have a tremendous capacity for application – though generally for fairly short periods at a time.

21 SUNDAY
Moon Age Day 5   Moon Sign Pisces

Right now the emphasis is on acquisition and material pleasure. You want to have a good time and to spoil yourself if at all possible but there is a bit of a dichotomy here because you are still likely to be holding tight to the cash. Why not find things to do that are pleasurable but which cost you little or nothing financially?

22 MONDAY
Moon Age Day 6   Moon Sign Pisces

Difficulties could come along today because of excessive haste or an inclination to force issues that have not yet matured. Stay cool, calm and collected in all your dealings with the world, while at the same time carefully monitoring and planning for your next move. Patience is the key to your eventual success.

23 TUESDAY
Moon Age Day 7   Moon Sign Aries

This is the time of the month when it is possible for you to get your own way easily. Don't be afraid to put your personal point of view forward or to be as positive and out-going as your go-ahead zodiac sign allows you to be. The lunar high brings new incentives and a strong desire to make progress in any way you can.

24 WEDNESDAY
Moon Age Day 8   Moon Sign Aries

Today you can expect to be the centre of attention and to make your own luck as you go along. Routines are not your forte at the moment. Your main concern is to get the job done and move on to the next exciting event. Romantic interludes could crop up later in the day, maybe at the time you would least expect.

25 THURSDAY   *Moon Age Day 9   Moon Sign Taurus*

You should be right on form when it comes to practical tasks and your sense of purpose has rarely been better. However, it is important to recognise that you can never force others to do what you want, when you want it, and this realisation may leave you feeling quite frustrated. Beware of pushing too hard – you will find that you are up against immovable objects.

26 FRIDAY   *Moon Age Day 10   Moon Sign Taurus*

The focus is now quite firmly on communication at every level. You are likely to be chatting to anyone who is willing to listen to you and there are gains to be made from listening to what is being said in return. You show yourself to be cultured at the moment and you appear to be suave and sophisticated.

27 SATURDAY   *Moon Age Day 11   Moon Sign Gemini*

Keep your eyes open because a new hobby becomes a possibility now, especially since the winter weather means you cannot get out and about as much as you might wish. Creatively speaking, you are on top form and you may be able to put these talents to good use. Take care, though, to avoid errors creeping into a few of your efforts.

28 SUNDAY   *Moon Age Day 12   Moon Sign Gemini*

Exercise a little caution and try to avoid situations in which it seems as though you are chasing your tail. It's possible that some of the things you are pushing to get done are not actually all that urgent and you would benefit far more from a little relaxation in order to reduce your stress levels. Understanding this is sometimes a problem for Aries.

29 MONDAY   *Moon Age Day 13   Moon Sign Cancer*

Keep up the good work and let those around you know what you are made of. Arians can be especially brave at present and you inspire confidence in other people. Plans that have lain dormant for the last couple of weeks can now be put into practice. Friendship should be especially important later in the day.

30 TUESDAY   *Moon Age Day 14   Moon Sign Cancer*

Being too assertive, possibly at work, might get you into some hot water. Never mind, you also have sufficient charm at present to talk your way out of just about any situation you manage to create around you. Give yourself a pat on the back for thinking up a newer and better way to perform an old task.

31 WEDNESDAY   *Moon Age Day 15   Moon Sign Leo*

In terms of career situations it looks as though a high degree of good luck is coming your way. This will not appear totally of its own accord, so it would be sensible to make the right sort of overtures, particularly when you are dealing with superiors. You approach most areas of life with great confidence at this time.

February

2018

1 THURSDAY
Moon Age Day 16   Moon Sign Leo

The only thing that is needed to make Thursday go with a swing is a little optimism. This shouldn't be too difficult for you to manage, given the prevailing planetary trends. In social and romantic matters, you should certainly be on the ball. Avoid giving yourself over to issues that cannot have a positive resolution, though.

2 FRIDAY
Moon Age Day 17   Moon Sign Virgo

The end of the working week for many Arians marks a time when you cease to take many things quite as seriously as you have done across the last few days. Conforming to expectation in a romantic and social sense proves to be quite easy and there is little doubt about your popularity now. Get out on the town this evening.

3 SATURDAY
Moon Age Day 18   Moon Sign Virgo

You may be forced to rely on your own resources today and will be happiest when you are making your own decisions. There are times when you need to rely on that Aries common sense, together with a little intuition and today is such a period. Friends should be helpful and kind and there are likely to be compliments coming your way.

4 SUNDAY
Moon Age Day 19   Moon Sign Libra

Beware because a sudden brake is put on your activities and progress as the monthly lunar low comes along. There is nothing else for it but to watch and wait for a while. Launching any new enterprise is not to be considered today or tomorrow. Consolidate your position and be willing to bide your time.

5 MONDAY
Moon Age Day 20   Moon Sign Libra

The Moon is in your opposite zodiac sign and this means that you should not take on matters that are going to tax you too much. Your confidence may be lacking, but you can get enjoyment from simple things and from the company of those you love. Shelve your plans if you can and enjoy some rest.

6 TUESDAY
Moon Age Day 21   Moon Sign Libra

Beware of just a little confusion today, although take comfort from the fact that this should not last long and you will soon be able to see clearly ahead again. You are likely to stumble if you rely a little too much on what others are telling you and fail to look at the evidence before your eyes, so take time to focus on issues carefully and think them through.

7 WEDNESDAY
Moon Age Day 22   Moon Sign Scorpio

Changes might be necessary at home if you want to make yourself more comfortable and also satisfy the needs family members have of you. At times it will be difficult to reconcile the views of everyone but this is something you can manage to do, just as long as you are willing to listen carefully.

8 THURSDAY
Moon Age Day 23   Moon Sign Scorpio

This could be the time to make gains as a result of communications that come your way. Keep an eye on the post and on email communications and react quickly when people get in touch with you. Conversations of all kinds are important under present trends, even if it seems that the subject under discussion is fairly inconsequential or pointless.

9 FRIDAY
Moon Age Day 24   Moon Sign Sagittarius

You won't wait around for anyone to make your luck for you today. On the contrary what you get from life is directly related to the amount of effort you are willing to put in. Although you might just tend to stay in the shadows in some ways, when it comes to cash you will be out there in the market place, haggling.

10 SATURDAY   *Moon Age Day 25   Moon Sign Sagittarius*

If the people who are stopping you in your tracks are not the sort of individuals to cross you as a rule, maybe they have a valid point. Aries can be very determined and certainly pushy, but that doesn't mean to say you are always right. Some of those you meet today might seem quite critical and you may have to accept their point of view.

11 SUNDAY   *Moon Age Day 26   Moon Sign Sagittarius*

You will be pleased to know that those in your home environment should be quite supportive at present and this is likely to lead to you choosing to spend time with friends and family today. You should find that you are quite happy to get away from the cut and thrust of the practical world, if only for a short while.

12 MONDAY   *Moon Age Day 27   Moon Sign Capricorn*

There's no doubt about it, this is definitely the best time to broaden your personal horizons. You can do this by carefully watching what is going on around you. Many of the ideas you have are a great deal better than those of people in your vicinity and convincing them that you know best ought to be a piece of cake if you remain calm.

13 TUESDAY   *Moon Age Day 28   Moon Sign Capricorn*

There is a calming influence today and pleasant experiences on the social front make for an entertaining time and should leave you feeling that life is more than worthwhile. Unfortunately, not everyone is in quite the frame of mind that you are and a degree of patience may be called for if you have to deal with people who simply don't share your happy mood.

14 WEDNESDAY   *Moon Age Day 29   Moon Sign Aquarius*

It is towards intimate relationships that you are presently turning your gaze – handy for Valentine's Day! – and it seems as though you have a great deal of influence regarding the thoughts and actions of loved ones. Money-wise, joint matters are on your mind at the moment and may remain that way for most of this day. There are gains to be made when you know where to look.

15 THURSDAY   *Moon Age Day 0   Moon Sign Aquarius*

For some Arians today there is suddenly a strong emphasis on personal security, together with a feeling for 'me' and 'mine' that seems to have come like a bolt from the blue. The fact is that this mood may have arisen from a lack of confidence, perhaps sparked by a casual word spoken by someone who didn't intend to stir up worries for you. Try to keep things in perspective.

16 FRIDAY   *Moon Age Day 1   Moon Sign Aquarius*

It should not be hard to get on well with others at this stage of the month and there are likely to be new individuals coming into your life under present astrological trends. Who knows, you might get to know someone famous, or else discover that a good friend is now about to enjoy a huge success? Love might come knocking later on today.

17 SATURDAY   *Moon Age Day 2   Moon Sign Pisces*

With the weekend comes a definite focus on your love life. If things have been getting a little routine, now is the time to increase the pace and to make things interesting. Don't stay at home this weekend if you have the chance to take a journey and, if at all possible, make it a romantic one. You might find that you receive some interesting proposals.

18 SUNDAY   *Moon Age Day 3   Moon Sign Pisces*

Leisure and entertainment are right up your street today. Not everyone shares your enthusiasm for having a good time so do be careful how much pressure you put on those around you when it comes to joining in. Refuse to be bullied by anyone today – even valued and loved family members.

19 MONDAY   *Moon Age Day 4   Moon Sign Aries*

The Moon returns to your own sign of Aries, bringing the lunar high for the month and filling you with confidence. This is the time to overthrow obstacles that might have existed and to make sure that what is happening around you is of your own choosing. You may struggle to have patience with others, so expect to be happiest doing your own thing.

20 TUESDAY
Moon Age Day 5   Moon Sign Aries

There is no reason why you should be restricted in any way today and it looks as though you are filled with enthusiasm from morning until night. Get to grips with tasks that might have seemed difficult in the recent past and see how easily you get through them now. Out of the ordinary situations are now more likely.

21 WEDNESDAY
Moon Age Day 6   Moon Sign Taurus

Most practical matters seem to be especially rewarding today. Pushing on for success, especially in professional matters, you give yourself readily to help the greater good once work is out of the way. There might be some time left over during which you can simply enjoy yourself, though probably not a great deal!

22 THURSDAY
Moon Age Day 7   Moon Sign Taurus

Attending to a variety of different sorts of interests is easy for you now. Avoid allowing yourself to become diverted by side issues and allow those close to you to take some of the strain if it seems important for them to do so. Ensure that the instructions you hand out to others, especially at work, are concise and easy to understand.

23 FRIDAY
Moon Age Day 8   Moon Sign Taurus

Prepare for some delays today, and these may lead you to worry about a specific project that is clearly on your mind. It doesn't matter how hard you push at the moment, trends suggest that you won't change anything. Better by far to understand this fact and be willing to wait patiently for matters to mature.

24 SATURDAY
Moon Age Day 9   Moon Sign Gemini

Socially speaking it is possible that you will be more reluctant to get involved in activities today than would normally be the case. You probably feel the urge to spend time on your own, or at least in the company of people who are close to you. This not a bad period for finding a warm fire and toasting your toes.

25 SUNDAY   *Moon Age Day 10   Moon Sign Gemini*

It's Sunday, so expect a relaxing sort of day, with plenty to divert you from the material considerations of life. You would probably enjoy spending time with friends and since you are so very sociable at the moment they in turn will relish the hours they spend with you. Today is about fun and not responsibility.

26 MONDAY   *Moon Age Day 11   Moon Sign Cancer*

At the start of a new working week for most, you can expect to begin a very productive period professionally. Getting to grips with issues that have bugged you for some time now seems to be a piece of cake. Meanwhile you find new friendships coming your way, together with a change in the emphasis of established relationships. Home and work matter equally to you at present.

27 TUESDAY   *Moon Age Day 12   Moon Sign Cancer*

This is a time when things definitely do work better in pairs. In business, or in romance, you are now happy to co-operate and to share confidences with others. Make the most of this spirit of partnership, and you should find that there are very few people who fail to fall under your spell.

28 WEDNESDAY   *Moon Age Day 13   Moon Sign Leo*

A change of scenery would do you the world of good, as would seeing some new faces, or at least those of people you haven't seen for quite some time. Make the most of any offers that come your way, especially social ones. Don't try to get through too much in a practical sense, even though you should feel physically fit, and instead make time for pleasure.

March

2018

1 THURSDAY
Moon Age Day 14   Moon Sign Leo

Romantic and social activities are well accented today and this could help you to make the best possible impression on all manner of people. There is also something quite unusual about this part of the month because you may start to notice how many strange coincidences begin to crop up, often at very opportune times.

2 FRIDAY
Moon Age Day 15   Moon Sign Virgo

You might find yourself in conflict with your partner or a family member at some stage today but things really don't have to be that way. Don't insist on putting your point of view across first but instead listen to what is being said to you. There is a possibility that you are misconstruing things and another careful look at matters would help.

3 SATURDAY
Moon Age Day 16   Moon Sign Virgo

There are likely to be plenty of discussions going on today, particularly with loved ones. You can gain some great insights by reading between the lines and by turning your intuition up to full. People generally could be saying one thing but feeling another and it is up to you at this time to tell the difference.

4 SUNDAY
Moon Age Day 17   Moon Sign Libra

The lunar low finds you out of sorts and less able to push forward in the way you like to. Splitting jobs might work well. At least this would mean you don't have the time to get bored, something that is quite likely to happen otherwise. The only real problem with today is that things don't go quite as you would wish.

5 MONDAY
Moon Age Day 18   Moon Sign Libra

It probably will not be possible to get to some appointments or to achieve the level of work that you would like today. Since you have most likely been making singular progress across the last couple of weeks you can afford to sit back and watch for a while. It might even prove to be advantageous to look at things from the touchline.

6 TUESDAY
Moon Age Day 19   Moon Sign Scorpio

Your larger-than-life Arian personality means that you just cannot help dominating events today. You are filled with enthusiasm and anxious to get going. If some of your colleagues or friends are slightly more cautious, they might be in for a hard time because you cannot wait around for them to catch up and will go it alone if necessary.

7 WEDNESDAY
Moon Age Day 20   Moon Sign Scorpio

Aries is now in an amorous frame of mind. The area of love and romance is favourably highlighted and you should find that the people you are fondest of are the ones who are showing you the greatest amount of attention. It won't always be possible to get your own way, even when you turn on the charm, but you can cause a stir.

8 THURSDAY
Moon Age Day 21   Moon Sign Sagittarius

Although you are very persuasive, an important discussion might fail to bring you exactly what you want, which will not please you after a few days during which you have become used to getting your own way. Some compromise might be necessary and could actually lead to a greater measure of success than you were originally hoping for.

9 FRIDAY
Moon Age Day 22   Moon Sign Sagittarius

You are very versatile at the moment and you can now put some of this quality to good use, particularly at work. When you are away from the professional arena, you should notice that personal attachments seem somewhat more rewarding and offer you incentives to be as kind as you can be to someone who really counts in your life.

10 SATURDAY   *Moon Age Day 23   Moon Sign Sagittarius*

Extra effort is put into those jobs you really favour, maybe at the expense of tasks you don't really want to undertake at all. This is a recurring theme during the present period and has to be guarded against. You can now be the star attraction in a social sense at the beginning of the weekend.

11 SUNDAY   *Moon Age Day 24   Moon Sign Capricorn*

It might be a mistake to take on too many diverse interests today, especially as this is a Sunday, which is supposed to be a day of rest. You work extremely hard and often push yourself more than is necessary, so when the planets allow for a little R and R, perhaps you should listen. You would be happiest today when surrounded by only a few people.

12 MONDAY   *Moon Age Day 25   Moon Sign Capricorn*

Pursuing new educational or cultural matters would seem to be appropriate at this time but you can turn your mind in almost any direction you wish. Keep in mind that pointless rules and regulations will not go down well with you at the moment, and you may even become resentful of them. All the same, you feel adventurous and optimistic, with a need for freedom.

13 TUESDAY   *Moon Age Day 26   Moon Sign Aquarius*

You should be able to keep up a varied and highly stimulating love life right now. Typical of you, there are not enough hours in the day to fit in everything you would wish to do but if you are selective you should discover opportunities that had not occurred to you before. Your finances may strengthen around now.

14 WEDNESDAY   *Moon Age Day 27   Moon Sign Aquarius*

As is usually the case, your mind is both quick and sharp, with a biting wit that can catch almost anyone off guard. Most of what you say goes right to the mark but take care that you do not upset one or two people unintentionally. If you keep your level of sarcasm down to about half of what it naturally seems to be today, things should work out fine.

15 THURSDAY   *Moon Age Day 28   Moon Sign Aquarius*

Stand by for a stronger emphasis on communication today. It is very important to make sure that you are getting your message across as successfully as you can. Take one job at a time, instead of the hundred you normally take on. It is important to specialise at this stage of the month and to make sure that each task is concluded before starting another.

16 FRIDAY   *Moon Age Day 29   Moon Sign Pisces*

You are now in something of a transitional phase, which may interfere with your decision-making process. Actually, this is a good time for change because you can get yourself into a frame of mind that enables you to take chances. Aries is a natural gambler, and for once this tendency pays off.

17 SATURDAY   *Moon Age Day 0   Moon Sign Pisces*

A small break from the norm would be sufficient to bring a degree of interest to your life. Saturday could demand extra effort at work but it is in the social arena that you are at your most potent. Don't be surprised if your popularity is high, with a number of important friends seeking you out.

18 SUNDAY   *Moon Age Day 1   Moon Sign Aries*

Along comes the lunar high and for the next two days you should be extremely positive in your approach and well able to get ahead, especially in a financial sense. Lady Luck should be on your side when it matters and since chancing your arm now seems to be second nature, you won't hesitate and can make real gains as a result.

19 MONDAY   *Moon Age Day 2   Moon Sign Aries*

You should now be turning all that positive power towards impressing people. At work you will shine out like a bright star and practically everything that you say today should seem to be inspired. Not everyone can keep up with your thought processes and there might be times today when it will be necessary to go it alone.

20 TUESDAY
Moon Age Day 3   Moon Sign Aries

You will need to take great care in professional matters, relying only on your own judgement and that of people you know you can trust. Be rather circumspect about spilling the beans regarding a specific topic to people who are outsiders. If in doubt it would definitely be better to keep secrets for now.

21 WEDNESDAY
Moon Age Day 4   Moon Sign Taurus

For today at least you could find yourself being rather more impressionable than might normally be the case. Try not to be over sensitive to the statements and opinions of others. If situations arise in which disputes are the norm, stay away from them, at least for the moment.

22 THURSDAY
Moon Age Day 5   Moon Sign Taurus

Certain delays are likely now and you will have to exercise a degree of patience when it comes to getting exactly what you want. Be prepared to think on your feet and to rearrange matters at a moment's notice. By remaining flexible you stay ahead of the game and can easily make some fairly startling gains.

23 FRIDAY
☿ *Moon Age Day 6   Moon Sign Gemini*

Stick around familiar faces and places, at least for the moment. You won't be quite as inclined today to take chances, and in any case your personal life is going to demand more of your time. This is no bad thing because a busy spell of late may well have prevented you from concentrating on romantic attachments.

24 SATURDAY
☿ *Moon Age Day 7   Moon Sign Gemini*

A firmer sense of personal and emotional security is now in view. Intimate relationships benefit greatly from these trends and those you love the most should give you renewed reasons for feeling extremely happy. Of course it isn't a one-way street because you are being very reassuring yourself.

25 SUNDAY   ☿   *Moon Age Day 8   Moon Sign Cancer*

Joint efforts benefit from some extra incentive today and it is therefore possible that you will harness your own capabilities to those of others. There is a good deal to be gained from any sort of co-operation this Sunday, though you must also remember that all work and no play will turn you into a dull Aries.

26 MONDAY   ☿   *Moon Age Day 9   Moon Sign Cancer*

The potential for success is strong, the only real stumbling block being the ability to keep your friends working so keenly on your behalf. Where practical and financial projects are concerned, you are going to have to find some way to convince people that they are working towards their own betterment too.

27 TUESDAY   ☿   *Moon Age Day 10   Moon Sign Leo*

Today you have the ability to charm those higher up the ladder of life to give you a hand up. Some Arians will be offered additional responsibilities at this time and are unlikely to turn down the opportunity. Conforming to expectations in a social sense isn't easy, but people are relying on you.

28 WEDNESDAY ☿   *Moon Age Day 11   Moon Sign Leo*

Although it would be presumptuous to suggest that you could do anything, this is certainly how you feel at times today. If not everything is going your way, it is probably because you are not trying hard enough. Bringing people round to your point of view is as easy as falling off a log now, so put your powers of persuasion to good use.

29 THURSDAY   ☿   *Moon Age Day 12   Moon Sign Virgo*

Now is the time to genuinely assess what is going on in your life and to make a few necessary minor alterations, especially with regard to professional matters. There is the possibility that you will meet people from the past, some of whom could have a fairly important part to play in your thinking for the future.

30 FRIDAY ☿ *Moon Age Day 13 Moon Sign Virgo*

Others may seem to lack the warmth you are seeking from them today. Maybe this is something to do with your own attitude, or an indication that you are looking in the wrong direction. When it comes to the practical aspects of life, you cope extremely well today, and continue to do so for some days.

31 SATURDAY ☿ *Moon Age Day 14 Moon Sign Libra*

Try to avoid any tendency to believe that the grass is greener on the other side of the fence. What you have and the way you deal with it should be enough for this Saturday, since you are not exactly firing on all cylinders at present. Gains can be made later in the day, probably as a result of loving attachments.

April

2018

1 SUNDAY ☿ Moon Age Day 15 Moon Sign Libra

It could appear that everyone else is getting ahead better than you are, which might partly explain your attitude of yesterday. This is now replaced by a feeling that you are being left behind, but it is only the lunar low at work. Counteract it by keeping busy, but don't expect too many startling successes.

2 MONDAY ☿ Moon Age Day 16 Moon Sign Scorpio

There ought to be time at the moment to salvage some valuable efforts from the past that, for one reason or another, did not work out well before. An idea that you had to put on hold can now be revisited and there should be opportunities to prove to the world how sound your thinking and your judgements actually are.

3 TUESDAY ☿ Moon Age Day 17 Moon Sign Scorpio

Aries needs to be heard at the moment and this can make you somewhat outspoken. As long as you can back your arguments with common sense and show that you know practical ways to get things done, all should be well. If you fail at all today it will be because you didn't think enough before deciding to act.

4 WEDNESDAY ☿ Moon Age Day 18 Moon Sign Scorpio

Relationships are especially important today, both in terms of positive and sometimes slightly negative influences. Although you are willing to look at all points of view, someone you always consider sensible may now appear to behave in a less than typical way. Exercise some patience and get to the bottom of any specific issue.

5 THURSDAY   ☿ *Moon Age Day 19*   *Moon Sign Sagittarius*

Keep pushing towards your objectives and allow yourself the right to be correct in most of your judgements. Your thought processes are as quick as lightning and you have plenty to offer the world in terms of your personality and intellect. Don't be afraid to say what you think because people are willing to accept your opinions now.

6 FRIDAY   ☿ *Moon Age Day 20*   *Moon Sign Sagittarius*

Careful planning allows you to get through potentially difficult circumstances, possibly without registering them until later. While others splash around in the shallow end of life, Aries likes to be out there with the adults. This is particularly the case at the moment and although you are very capable, you can sometimes push too hard.

7 SATURDAY   ☿ *Moon Age Day 21*   *Moon Sign Capricorn*

How about a spot of recycling? Today's trends point to making something good out of something you would usually discard. This does not simply relate to material possessions but also to the way you think. Look again at a long-lost idea and see how possible it would be to put it into a new jacket and to get it working in the world once more.

8 SUNDAY   ☿ *Moon Age Day 22*   *Moon Sign Capricorn*

A great deal of planetary energy is now likely to be focused on your own needs and requirements. Like all Fire signs, Aries can have a slightly selfish streak from time to time, although at the moment it appears that you help others as much as you do yourself. Confidence is not hard to find in personal matters and forward progress is obvious.

9 MONDAY   ☿ *Moon Age Day 23*   *Moon Sign Capricorn*

In a practical sense, work hard today to give yourself a break later. Meanwhile, taking chances in romantic situations could lead to a few complications and so really isn't worthwhile. It is true that you enjoy a good deal of popularity at present, which is generally the case, if you push situations too far you could create problems as a result.

10 TUESDAY ☿ *Moon Age Day 24   Moon Sign Aquarius*

You should now be pretty much on top of the world and anxious to make the most of whatever life is offering. This is more than can be said for someone at home or perhaps a very good friend. With so much energy to spare you can afford to slow things down just a little in order to listen and to offer the sound advice of which you are so capable.

11 WEDNESDAY ☿ *Moon Age Day 25   Moon Sign Aquarius*

A slightly aggravating situation could develop today. You may be at loggerheads in a friendship and if this is the case, it really would be sensible to stand back and look at things in a different way, rather than slogging it out with someone you actually like very much. To retreat from such a situation is not a sign of defeat but rather a mark of your intelligence.

12 THURSDAY ☿ *Moon Age Day 26   Moon Sign Pisces*

Today it may not be easy to conform to the expectations of others because the fact is that sometimes you disagree with those expectations. Balance can be hard to find but it's important if you really want to achieve. Give everyone a fair hearing at this time, even individuals who might appear to have let you down somehow in the past.

13 FRIDAY ☿ *Moon Age Day 27   Moon Sign Pisces*

What a joyful soul you are today. Your attitude towards life invokes optimism in others, which in turn leads them to help you. There are gains coming from a number of different directions at the moment and you ought to find that romance is particularly well accented. An offer from friends might prove too good to miss – so go for it!

14 SATURDAY ☿ *Moon Age Day 28   Moon Sign Pisces*

Make sure that you pass on good news today and ensure that those with whom you come into contact understand the implications of what you are telling them. There ought to be plenty of gossip around at the moment and whilst you don't usually deal in rumours, you probably cannot avoid doing so under present planetary trends.

15 SUNDAY
Moon Age Day 29   Moon Sign Aries

Use your intuition to the full and go for gold in anything you decide to take on at this time. There is room for great confidence and a rising tide of determination that typifies your Fire-sign nature. Some natural good luck should put you in a position of power, most likely regarding practical issues.

16 MONDAY
Moon Age Day 0   Moon Sign Aries

What an excellent start to a working week this should turn out to be. With the lunar high around you will be taking some of the thoughts you had across the weekend and putting them into practice. Now is definitely the right time to make progress and there ought to be plenty of people around who will be only too happy to share in the reflective glory.

17 TUESDAY
Moon Age Day 1   Moon Sign Taurus

A very curious attitude takes you over during this part of April. Suddenly you want to know why things work in the way they do. This applies to mechanical gadgets, but is just as applicable to relationships and friendships. All the same, you need to learn that it isn't necessary to take everything to pieces simply on the grounds of curiosity.

18 WEDNESDAY
Moon Age Day 2   Moon Sign Taurus

You are now entering a period of escapism. This isn't all that common for Aries so you need to take care not to neglect important jobs that you have already started. All the same there is nothing wrong with being a dreamer now and again. You might even arrive at some startling conclusions.

19 THURSDAY
Moon Age Day 3   Moon Sign Gemini

Work and career issues today may be something of a chore today. Routines really don't move you very much at the moment and what you need is some change in your life. Keep abreast of current affairs and, when circumstances allow, indulge in a good chat with people you find attractive and interesting.

20 FRIDAY
Moon Age Day 4   Moon Sign Gemini

You may find it relatively easy to handle several different tasks at the same time today. Don't allow yourself to be diverted from paths you know to be right for you and insist on getting your own way on those occasions when you just know that your intuition is sound. Look out for kind words coming your way later in the day.

21 SATURDAY
Moon Age Day 5   Moon Sign Cancer

There are great opportunities around now for broadening your horizons in a general sense. Whether or not you choose to act on these opportunities remains to be seen. Certainly the better weather will encourage you to get out of the house and journeys of all sorts are well highlighted in your chart at present.

22 SUNDAY
Moon Age Day 6   Moon Sign Cancer

Unfortunately you appear to be totally uncompromising today. This is a state of mind that overtakes Aries from time to time. As long as you balance this tendency with a willingness to at least see the other person's point of view all should be well. On a positive note, it's amazing how much you can do in a practical sense today.

23 MONDAY
Moon Age Day 7   Moon Sign Leo

The chance to co-operate with a number of different people at the moment could prove very fruitful. On a business front you are now having new ideas that are both inspirational and fun, while you are also likely to experience some unexpected popularity when in social situations. Make the best of both worlds.

24 TUESDAY
Moon Age Day 8   Moon Sign Leo

Your power and influence are certainly not in doubt today. Use the force of your personality sparingly because a little goes a long way right now. From a financial point of view, it appears you have some very good ideas. It is possible you will make yourself better off by the weekend.

25 WEDNESDAY   *Moon Age Day 9   Moon Sign Virgo*

Find something that you can accomplish today and get cracking just as hard as you can. This is not likely to be a particularly restful day, but it ought to be very interesting. Social outings, either during the day or in the evening, leave you feeling quite contented and happy with your lot.

26 THURSDAY   *Moon Age Day 10   Moon Sign Virgo*

This is a time for pleasantries, particularly where your general social life is concerned. Arians who are not involved in a permanent romantic attachment should keep their eyes open at present, and even those who are in a relationship can expect a greater than average share of positive attention from the world at large as the positive trends rub off.

27 FRIDAY   *Moon Age Day 11   Moon Sign Virgo*

In group situations especially, there appears to be a good deal to keep you happy at present. You may be getting somewhat tired of certain routines, and probably feel you need a rest. The stars cannot promise that, but what they do indicate is a gradual but radical change of emphasis that is nearly as good.

28 SATURDAY   *Moon Age Day 12   Moon Sign Libra*

You can either use the lunar low to your advantage or worry about the fact that things seem to be out of control. In some situations, when there is nothing you can do, the best thing to do is nothing. Aries finds it difficult to think this way but you can afford to trust providence to look after you for short periods of time and this is one of them.

29 SUNDAY   *Moon Age Day 13   Moon Sign Libra*

Take advantage of the offer of some quality time that you can spend with your partner, or maybe even members of the family. It is true that you may not be quite as busy at work or practical sense as is sometimes the case. However, everyone needs a break, even the average Aries.

30 MONDAY
Moon Age Day 14   Moon Sign Scorpio

Though career demands will be the main priority of most Arians at present, don't leave matters associated with love on the back burner. The truth is that relationships count for a great deal at this time. Friends may well be demanding some of your time and you should easily be able to find moments to fit them in.

May

2018

1 TUESDAY
Moon Age Day 15   Moon Sign Scorpio

Current planetary trends make it easy to get what you want with others. People should be more than willing to put themselves out on your behalf and it appears that you have everything in place to move forward progressively. However, if you sign up to any social contracts you should look at them carefully.

2 WEDNESDAY
Moon Age Day 16   Moon Sign Sagittarius

You can gain a great deal today from approaching matters analytically, and making proper preparations before you begin. Some people around you might be taking chances but that is unlikely to be the case for you right now. Your attitude towards love and romance tends to be casual for the moment – or at least that is how it might appear.

3 THURSDAY
Moon Age Day 17   Moon Sign Sagittarius

Expect a good deal of nervous energy right now and make sure that in between all your efforts you find time to get some rest. Fire signs such as yours often tend to think they can go on more or less forever without any sort of break but this is not the case at all. Do something that feeds your intellect once the responsibilities of the day are finished.

4 FRIDAY
Moon Age Day 18   Moon Sign Sagittarius

It is really important now to listen to what other people have to say. There could be a tendency for you to assume that you know best about most matters. In many cases you will be right but that is no reason to ignore input from other directions. People will respect you much more if you bear what they have to say in mind and incorporate their views.

5 SATURDAY   *Moon Age Day 19   Moon Sign Capricorn*

Offers of co-operation may surround you, even when you think it would be best to go it alone. If you turn away from the very real help that is on offer you could be doing yourself a disservice. Aries often assumes it knows best and although in most cases this is probably true there are occasions when you can make life less complicated by accepting the help that's on offer.

6 SUNDAY   *Moon Age Day 20   Moon Sign Capricorn*

This is a part of the year during which you will be constantly growing in experience and knowledge. It isn't really the practical side of life that occupies you most but rather theoretical notions. You know instinctively that you have to try things out in your mind before you choose to put them into practice in the real world.

7 MONDAY   *Moon Age Day 21   Moon Sign Aquarius*

Your mind is now filled with ideas and you have boundless energy with which to put some of them into practice. You are likely to be flavour of the month in social settings and it appears that you have some special admirers at this time. People from the past are likely to reappear and you are likely to enjoy a little nostalgia.

8 TUESDAY   *Moon Age Day 22   Moon Sign Aquarius*

It is entirely likely that a slight shift in emphasis will bring you to an outdoor frame of mind, which bearing in mind the advancing year is probably not so much of a surprise. You will also be quite intellectually motivated and anxious to travel to places that have a strong historical bias and which retain a strong atmosphere of the past.

9 WEDNESDAY   *Moon Age Day 23   Moon Sign Aquarius*

If you have been sensible recently, you will have just a little cash to spare and can use it to invest wisely. However, rash decisions should be avoided at all costs. Meanwhile, you should find that romantic offers are coming in thick and fast, and in some cases these are likely to arrive from unexpected directions. This would also be a great time to look at new hobbies.

10 THURSDAY
Moon Age Day 24   Moon Sign Pisces

Communication and the exchange of views seem particularly important to you now and you are slightly inclined to bulldoze your opinions more than is either necessary or wise. When you are at your Arian best there isn't a more popular or honourable person around and this is the individual for which you need to strive.

11 FRIDAY
Moon Age Day 25   Moon Sign Pisces

It is important to avoid unnecessary conflicts with others before the start of the weekend. There isn't much doubt that you will win any arguments in which you take part but you will probably only end up feeling bad about the situation. Better by far to stop such eventualities before they start. This would be a great time for a shopping spree.

12 SATURDAY
Moon Age Day 26   Moon Sign Aries

A large helping of good luck pushes you towards your objectives at the moment and makes it possible for you to take the odd chance. Because your level of popularity is now so high, you willingly take part in all manner of social encounters. This in turn increases your popularity and boosts your charisma. Make the best use of the lunar high.

13 SUNDAY
Moon Age Day 27   Moon Sign Aries

For most Arians the green light is on and it seems certain that you intend to push forward as hard and as fast as you can. With little to stand in your way, it is professional matters that show strongest in the glare of the lunar high this month. Don't take no for an answer and be willing to go that extra step if necessary.

14 MONDAY
Moon Age Day 28   Moon Sign Taurus

Keep listening in because there could be important discussions today, though you don't want them to turn into disputes and should make that fact as clear as you can, early in the day. If you have some test or examination in front of you, now is the time to start boning up on those all important questions. Concentration counts today.

15 TUESDAY   *Moon Age Day 0   Moon Sign Taurus*

There could be some limitations around, particularly in terms of love. Maybe the one you care about the most is unwilling to share their innermost feelings with you, or it could be possible that you find yourself the subject of a jealous outburst. It might simply be easier to spend as much time today as you can with friends and to leave other issues to simmer for a while.

16 WEDNESDAY   *Moon Age Day 1   Moon Sign Gemini*

There could be the odd emotional disappointment to be dealt with today, especially regarding your love life. These can be dealt with fairly easily just as long as you are willing to talk things through. An understanding attitude on your part also assists in curing an ill that goes back quite some time.

17 THURSDAY   *Moon Age Day 2   Moon Sign Gemini*

A day of positive ambitions comes along now. Aspects to your Sun favour decisive actions on your part. Other planetary alignments take care of popularity and put you very much in the winning seat today. There may be a way to go in specific projects but you are making ground all the time.

18 FRIDAY   *Moon Age Day 3   Moon Sign Cancer*

If you sense any sort of polarisation between home and career, you will simply have to find a way to split your time more equally. That won't necessarily be easy but it is very important to ensure that those you love know how you feel. There are ways to combine relationships and your work but not easily at present.

19 SATURDAY   *Moon Age Day 4   Moon Sign Cancer*

Things can now fall into place rather well in a career sense. You are willing to take a chance and also to speak your mind. Don't be left at the back of the field in any sort of competition and if you know this is likely to happen, avoid joining the race. Concentrate on those things for which you have a natural aptitude.

20 SUNDAY
Moon Age Day 5   Moon Sign Leo

There are rewarding times on the social scene ahead today and particularly so when you find yourself in the company of people you have always considered to be stimulating. With lots of compliments coming your way, and your popularity high, the only note of caution is that you should not allow your partner to become jealous!

21 MONDAY
Moon Age Day 6   Moon Sign Leo

Current trends indicate that it is easy for you to turn most situations in your own chosen direction. If you are beginning some new sort of routine, make certain that you have planned things out carefully first. Not everyone appears to have your best interests at heart but the people who really matter are on your side.

22 TUESDAY
Moon Age Day 7   Moon Sign Leo

A little luck is all you need to make something quite wonderful happen in your life. This is the day when it is most likely to come along. With the days lengthening, spring firmly in the air and everything potentially going your way it's time to get out there and make the world recognise your potential.

23 WEDNESDAY
Moon Age Day 8   Moon Sign Virgo

What you probably need most of all today is a total change from routine. Even if the weather is not great you would gain from being out of doors and from doing something that really pleases you. Stay in the company of those you really like and enjoy all the laughs that can come your way right now.

24 THURSDAY
Moon Age Day 9   Moon Sign Virgo

The time is now right to make sure you have your eyes and ears open because there is a good deal of fresh input coming along today. You might also feel the need for some fresh air and certainly will not take kindly to being cooped up all day long. A certain restless streak begins to develop.

25 FRIDAY   *Moon Age Day 10   Moon Sign Libra*

Vitality is likely to be in short supply today, a fact for which you can blame the lunar low. You just don't have the drive and enthusiasm that often concludes your working week and may find that you need to make excuses for this. Judge today and tomorrow as an interlude best suited to contemplation.

26 SATURDAY   *Moon Age Day 11   Moon Sign Libra*

You could end up in an undesirable situation if you put trust in the wrong people today, so it is vitally important that you take nothing at all for granted. Rather you should be more cautious than usual and ensure that you ask the most searching of questions, especially regarding contracts.

27 SUNDAY   *Moon Age Day 12   Moon Sign Scorpio*

Enjoying all that domestic relationships have to offer could prove somewhat more difficult than usual today. The fact is that you won't get on with everyone at home right now. It will seem from your point of view that someone is being distinctly difficult, but in reality it is possible you should be looking in the mirror.

28 MONDAY   *Moon Age Day 13   Moon Sign Scorpio*

This is a time when you will benefit from broadening your intellectual and social interests. Trips for pleasure are indicated, particularly those of cultural interest. Arians who are not at work today will be the luckiest, making this a good candidate for a day off if you can swing it.

29 TUESDAY   *Moon Age Day 14   Moon Sign Sagittarius*

What a good time this would be for family gatherings of almost any sort. You are very sociable at present and can even put up cheerfully with the one or two difficult family members. Keep an open mind about a change in travel plans that might have a bearing on you later.

30 WEDNESDAY *Moon Age Day 15 Moon Sign Sagittarius*

Positive trends now fall in the area of work and finance. Make sure you don't push yourself too hard and never rely on your nerve, because, like everyone else in the world, you can go too far. It's hard to believe that fact at the moment but if you don't take some rest, you will discover the truth of the matter.

31 THURSDAY *Moon Age Day 16 Moon Sign Sagittarius*

The emphasis today is on the wider social world and it is just possible that your work will take something of a back seat. You probably have a few inspirational ideas in your head and will want to get them moving in the real world. It's a good idea to look for some support, and you should find it forthcoming.

June

2018

1 FRIDAY
Moon Age Day 17   Moon Sign Capricorn

At the moment, travel and cultural matters should be high on your personal agenda. It appears that the more refined qualities of your nature are showing themselves and you will want to demonstrate them to the world. If there is a mountain of jobs to be done, just deal with them steadily, one at a time.

2 SATURDAY
Moon Age Day 18   Moon Sign Capricorn

If you are willing to go with the flow and to co-operate with people who you instinctively trust, matters are apt to sort themselves out. This leaves you somewhat freer to get on with patching up a dent in an important relationship. Avoid becoming obsessed with any problem, particularly a work issue that it would be better to accept you cannot alter.

3 SUNDAY
Moon Age Day 19   Moon Sign Aquarius

Sharing is always best, and remembering this may help you if things go awry today. Bear in mind that you can accomplish anything with a little help from your friends. This is not a good time to go it alone and failure to recognise this could leave you in for a roller-coaster ride. Sharing the responsibility for mistakes is always a bonus, too!

4 MONDAY
Moon Age Day 20   Moon Sign Aquarius

If you have any problems today, take them to people you know. It seems as though you fare best when spending time with those you trust. The outside world can seem somehow unnerving at present, even though this is nothing but a temporary phase. Be willing to share a new idea with someone who expresses genuine interest.

5 TUESDAY
Moon Age Day 21   Moon Sign Aquarius

When it comes to popularity and making a good impression it appears that you are second to none now. It's time to make your move, whatever you want that to be. You are likely to be faced with a number of different potential directions and have rarely been in a better position to choose in which direction to go.

6 WEDNESDAY
Moon Age Day 22   Moon Sign Pisces

Arians should be open to innovation under present trends, and keen to find ways to make certain aspects of life easier. Friends and relatives alike prove to be very attentive now, but you are likely to be in a contemplative mood that could lead to the successful modification and streamlining of ideas.

7 THURSDAY
Moon Age Day 23   Moon Sign Pisces

Today offers plenty of opportunity to have fun and with some progressive trends showing up in your solar chart, now is a time to think about adventure. However, bear in mind that you will not be in the right frame of mind to do anything alone. You should take every possible opportunity to be with your friends now.

8 FRIDAY
Moon Age Day 24   Moon Sign Aries

Practical and professional situations move on relentlessly, but you are very much more in command than you might think. It could seem that the pressure is on in personal or domestic situations, which means talking more to family members and probably making a few concessions on the way.

9 SATURDAY
Moon Age Day 25   Moon Sign Aries

Keep an open mind about the way family members and even friends are behaving, while following your instinct to give most of your concentration to romantic attachments and the social delights they can offer. The planets suggest that you should keep your eyes and ears open for new input which is coming in with the lunar high.

10 SUNDAY   *Moon Age Day 26   Moon Sign Aries*

Aries is often extremely busy and in the hustle and bustle it is easy to forget to say the things that are important, especially where relationships are concerned. Kerb your sense of adventure today and focus on family and your partner. Someone really needs your assistance today and as it's Sunday you may have plenty of time to attend to them.

11 MONDAY   *Moon Age Day 27   Moon Sign Taurus*

It should be obvious today that the present planetary trends are making it hard for you to think clearly. For this reason, you should be willing to seek out the impartial advice of good friends, or people who are experts in their own given fields. After all, you can't excel at everything, even if you would wish to.

12 TUESDAY   *Moon Age Day 28   Moon Sign Taurus*

You probably have a few inspirational ideas in your head and will want to get some of them moving in the real world. You could do worse than to look for some support right now. The emphasis today is on the wider social world and it is just possible that your work will take something of a back seat.

13 WEDNESDAY   *Moon Age Day 0   Moon Sign Gemini*

You will have little patience with mundane tasks today and may wish to spend at least part of the weekend doing exactly what takes your fancy. There is no problem with this way of thinking, just as long as the really essential tasks are taken care of before you turn your attention in different directions.

14 THURSDAY   *Moon Age Day 1   Moon Sign Gemini*

You are unlikely to be thwarted today once you have made up your mind to a particular course of action. You know what you want from life and have a very good idea how to get it. Your typical Arian traits are definitely in evidence, and continue to be so for the whole of the day and beyond.

15 FRIDAY
Moon Age Day 2   Moon Sign Cancer

Trifling matters and small obligations will keep you busy through most of today, which is exactly why you want to let your hair down when the evening comes around. All sorts of new interests take your fancy but once you have set your mind on a particular activity you will throw yourself into it wholeheartedly.

16 SATURDAY
Moon Age Day 3   Moon Sign Cancer

If you have documents to sign at present, read the small print carefully. You may be feeling bold and quite keen to take a few chances. That is fine, just as long as the risks are calculated carefully. If necessary, talk your options through with someone impartial before you go ahead, and never, ever take a financial risk that you cannot afford.

17 SUNDAY
Moon Age Day 4   Moon Sign Leo

The planets suggest that you might be inclined to be over-assertive today – and that won't help many situations. Try to remain as humble as possible because that is the way you are most likely to influence those around you. In a practical sense, a little of this and a bit of that is the way to approach jobs at present.

18 MONDAY
Moon Age Day 5   Moon Sign Leo

Pay close attention to any new ideas coming to you from the outside world. Even the smallest pieces of information can be used to bolster your own ideas and there are some important lessons to be learned. Romance is high on your agenda for today, even if you don't at first realise it, so make time for loved ones later in the day.

19 TUESDAY
Moon Age Day 6   Moon Sign Virgo

Some tension is likely to develop in emotional relationships as the week goes on, so start on a positive note by keeping things light and airy. Deep and meaningful discussions are probably not a good idea because of their tendency to end with disagreements. If conflict does seem likely, perhaps take time out to spend with friends.

20 WEDNESDAY *Moon Age Day 7   Moon Sign Virgo*

Along comes a boost and a time when mundane matters seem to look after themselves while you set your mind on having a good time. Attitude is all-important when dealing with personal relationships and you should find yourself able to adopt just the right tone to both impress and to educate someone.

21 THURSDAY *Moon Age Day 8   Moon Sign Libra*

There will be plenty of time to get on with what you want later so for now, take a well-earned rest. Don't press the action button of your life too much at this time but instead allow situations to wash over you, even if this is not something you would usually do and to do so seems somehow tedious.

22 FRIDAY *Moon Age Day 9   Moon Sign Libra*

Don't expect everything in life to suit you today, although it is true that the majority of situations should do so. Routines may be hard to establish and, all things considered, you should be happy to go with the flow. What matters most to you right now is your rising popularity.

23 SATURDAY *Moon Age Day 10   Moon Sign Scorpio*

A brisker time socially finds you flitting gregariously from one situation to another. The planets suggest, however, that you could gain a great deal from taking the time to listen to what is being said by those around you. The attitude of a particular friend could be somewhat difficult to understand but if you pay attention things can be sorted out quite easily.

24 SUNDAY *Moon Age Day 11   Moon Sign Scorpio*

The positive social trend continues, and it should become increasingly easy to get along with people who were difficult a few days ago. Routines can be tiresome, which is exactly why you tend to ignore them if you can. Artistically you are on top form so perhaps this is a good time to plan changes at home.

25 MONDAY   *Moon Age Day 12   Moon Sign Scorpio*

You now enter a period of reorganisation but it's important not to allow opportunities to slip through your fingers just because you are busy trying to do a dozen things at once. Stop, look and listen – this is the best advice for this period and seems to be particularly applicable today.

26 TUESDAY   *Moon Age Day 13   Moon Sign Sagittarius*

Others should find you interesting and stimulating to have around, a fact that helps you no end in your general path through life this Tuesday. Although not a generally inspirational sort of day, this one has much to offer at work and, after that, socially. Your confidence is gradually on the increase, too.

27 WEDNESDAY *Moon Age Day 14   Moon Sign Sagittarius*

Your powers of attraction are definitely strengthening at the moment, so use them to the full. No matter what the weather happens to be doing you may feel the need of some fresh air and a positive change of scene. Accept that it is not possible to get all practical matters out of the way at the same time and pace yourself.

28 THURSDAY   *Moon Age Day 15   Moon Sign Capricorn*

Social matters and general encounters with others should prove to be both rewarding and interesting today. Be careful you don't cause inadvertent offence to colleagues, although you don't go too far the other way into obsequiousness either. Compromise is an important word today but so is integrity.

29 FRIDAY   *Moon Age Day 16   Moon Sign Capricorn*

You should be on a fairly easy path towards your objectives today and may gain a great deal from simply being in the right place at the right time. Enjoy what life has to offer but remember that you achieve the most now when you complete every job before beginning the next.

30 SATURDAY   *Moon Age Day 17   Moon Sign Capricorn*

There is much of interest going on in the outside world and today you won't be at the back of the queue when it comes to joining in. With plenty of energy, more than a smattering of good luck and an instinctive understanding of how to behave, you can make this a real day to remember.

July

2018

1 SUNDAY
Moon Age Day 18   Moon Sign Aquarius

Make sure you don't rely too heavily on your nerves because, like everyone else in the world, you can go too far. It might be hard to believe this at the moment, but if you don't take some rest you will discover the truth of the matter. Positive trends now fall in the area of work and financial developments generally.

2 MONDAY
Moon Age Day 19   Moon Sign Aquarius

Give yourself a pat on the back for recent successes at work but do not allow these to go to your head. There is still plenty to do if you want to get exactly where you need to be. You will want to be on the move today and so will not take kindly to any situation that ties you exclusively to a particular spot.

3 TUESDAY
Moon Age Day 20   Moon Sign Pisces

You won't be stuck for something to do socially, but there are times today when you could become bored with the same old routines. Favourable domestic relationships make it easier for you to concentrate on practical matters, without spending too much time sorting out the problems of your family.

4 WEDNESDAY
Moon Age Day 21   Moon Sign Pisces

Leaving situations to chance won't work half as well as preparing yourself for all eventualities in advance and there is plenty of help around if you are willing to ask the right questions. Conforming to the expectations others have of you could prove somewhat difficult later in the day. Success comes today if you are properly organised.

5 THURSDAY   *Moon Age Day 22   Moon Sign Pisces*

Although the things others want you to do will sometimes go against the grain, in the main you are likely to enjoy the cut and thrust of a busy and eventful social life. You may feel especially warmly towards family members, too. There is enough happening on the personal and domestic scene to keep you happy and fulfilled right now.

6 FRIDAY   *Moon Age Day 23   Moon Sign Aries*

This is the most progressive and rewarding part of the month. It seems as though all your energy has returned on the same day and it is highly unlikely that anything will hold you back for long. Countering the slightly negative remarks and attitude of particular friends ought to be quite easy if it is necessary at this time.

7 SATURDAY   *Moon Age Day 24   Moon Sign Aries*

You can talk almost anyone into anything at this time, though you may choose to focus on people who you feel have been taking a somewhat shaky path of late. In addition, you are funny and very resourceful. Altogether, this is a winning combination and with the lunar high around you have everything to play for.

8 SUNDAY   *Moon Age Day 25   Moon Sign Taurus*

Social trends are especially rewarding so enjoy spending time in the company of good friends. Sporting events of any kind are ideal, or perhaps a total change of scene and a journey of some sort. Today has the potential to be very rewarding but you do need to be careful about which areas of life you choose to highlight.

9 MONDAY   *Moon Age Day 26   Moon Sign Taurus*

With abundant energy and the progressive nature of recent trends still in your mind and showing in your actions, you demonstrate a powerful impulse to do things right. Your social conscience is very definitely pricked at this time, and much of what you choose to accomplish may be on behalf of others.

10 TUESDAY
Moon Age Day 27   Moon Sign Gemini

Concentrate on enjoying yourself and find ways to cheer up those who are less happy at present. This is an excellent time to let the world know what a big personality you have. Stay away from those who seem to have it in their minds to throw a spanner in the works for you, or at the very least refuse to rise to their bait.

11 WEDNESDAY
Moon Age Day 28   Moon Sign Gemini

You need to realise today that everyone has their own song to sing, which is fine as long as you go on humming your own, too. There may be some undue pressure put upon you, most likely in the workplace. Avoid any temptation to overreact and this should be like water off a duck's back.

12 THURSDAY
Moon Age Day 29   Moon Sign Cancer

Don't push yourself harder than is necessary at this point in time because your social trends are looking good and it might be pleasant to spend at least a few hours today simply finding ways to enjoy yourself. Other trends suggest that a good percentage of your time will doubtless be taken up thinking about practical matters, especially money.

13 FRIDAY
Moon Age Day 0   Moon Sign Cancer

You are likely to find yourself thinking deeply and pondering matters more carefully than would usually be the case and you may even surprise yourself with your sensitivity. It's almost as if you can feel the way others are thinking and predict their likely actions and responses. A calm, contemplative Aries is now on display.

14 SATURDAY
Moon Age Day 1   Moon Sign Leo

Your confidence is especially high and you have exactly what it takes to get ahead on several different fronts at the same time. Expect to be the centre of attention but don't do anything to incite jealousy in others. Today may offer a way out of a certain trap that you have set for yourself recently.

15 SUNDAY
Moon Age Day 2   Moon Sign Leo

Today is especially good for planning ahead and for talking to friends and family members alike. Concern for the underdog is also evident – not always a common trait for Arians. This is a day on which you are likely to find it harder to get ahead than would usually be the case, so pace yourself and don't push matters further than it is possible to go.

16 MONDAY
Moon Age Day 3   Moon Sign Virgo

Friendships have a lot going for them today and it is possible that you will be associating with someone you haven't seen for quite some time. The planets suggest that although you can't put the clock back, you might now decide that you want to put something right that you blamed yourself for earlier.

17 TUESDAY
Moon Age Day 4   Moon Sign Virgo

Keeping things on an even keel in a practical sense may not be easy today. Try to stay cool, even when you think there is provocation from someone nearby. The consternation of a friend or a family member can usually be sorted out quite easily, so take the time to help others if you see your assistance is needed.

18 WEDNESDAY
Moon Age Day 5   Moon Sign Libra

The reason that you are experiencing a slight downturn can be summarised in three words: the lunar low. This is that time during which the Moon occupies the zodiac sign opposite to your own. You will simply have to settle for second best today, but take comfort from the knowledge that by tomorrow trends will be looking more progressive again.

19 THURSDAY
Moon Age Day 6   Moon Sign Libra

It would definitely be best to avoid arguments and be especially careful to stay away from sour grapes. If you put on a rational, cool and collected front you may ultimately get your own way in the end. Thanks in the main to the lunar low, today you may feel that others are getting ahead better than you are and this can be a cause of some distinct frustration.

20 FRIDAY
Moon Age Day 7   Moon Sign Libra

The lunar low is still in operation, preventing you from progressing in quite the way you would wish and perhaps taking some of the shine off a life that until the past few days had been jogging along nicely. If anything redresses the balance, it is the attitude of family members and, of course, your partner.

21 SATURDAY
Moon Age Day 8   Moon Sign Scorpio

Trends move on and place the focus on intimate relationships today. You are able to say just the right things to please people and may also find that friends are especially warm and helpful. A few strangers may be difficult to deal with but that's a small price to pay on what should otherwise be an ideal day.

22 SUNDAY
Moon Age Day 9   Moon Sign Scorpio

This is a good time to address some intensely personal issues and people will take you every bit as seriously as you take yourself. Conversation comes easily, as is often the case for Aries, and you might be in just the right place to benefit materially when it matters the most. A day for having fun.

23 MONDAY
Moon Age Day 10   Moon Sign Sagittarius

Take care not to overlook some of the little messages that are coming in at present. Trends put you in the mood to observe the game of life rather than participate in it, which might turn out to be something of a mistake. Routines won't be appealing and it might be fun to simply please yourself instead, especially in social situations.

24 TUESDAY
Moon Age Day 11   Moon Sign Sagittarius

Now is a good time to capitalise on any new opportunity that comes along. Do what you can to get important jobs out of the way, particularly if you have been making changes at home. Socially you need the cut and thrust of interaction with as many different people as you can possibly manage.

25 WEDNESDAY   *Moon Age Day 12   Moon Sign Capricorn*

The results of recent attempts to make changes in your life could be a very mixed bag. Now you are more circumspect and probably unwilling to take risks, especially with personal happiness. If something has been worrying you, this is the time to seek out a really good friend for some heartfelt advice.

26 THURSDAY   *Moon Age Day 13   Moon Sign Capricorn*

You are impatient to see your ideas becoming reality, but resist the temptation to rush any situation today. Take things slowly and steadily, making certain that you have dealt with every contingency. Creating the necessary mental space to dream some important dreams is another factor you can't dismiss today.

27 FRIDAY   *Moon Age Day 14   Moon Sign Capricorn*

With energy now definitely at a peak you are entering the most potentially successful time of the month. Be bold and brash because for the moment you can get away with it. Take the most important of your schemes and put them into practice. Socially speaking life should be looking especially good.

28 SATURDAY   *Moon Age Day 15   Moon Sign Aquarius*

Rewards may come via the broadening of your horizons and through travel. This would be an excellent time for Arians to take a holiday, or simply to get away from the everyday for a few hours. Almost any sort of journey would suit you, as long as it is undertaken for fun.

29 SUNDAY   *Moon Age Day 16   Moon Sign Aquarius*

The pursuit of outdoor interests could make the day go with a swing, particularly if you don't have to work. Although you are now quite competitive, this doesn't really extend to professional matters. With no real sense of ultimate responsibility at present, you really only want to have some fun.

30 MONDAY
Moon Age Day 17   Moon Sign Pisces

You can steal a march over your competitors in the workplace simply by being in the right place at the right time. Your ideas are good and those around you are more than willing to join in with them. Congratulations could be in order somewhere in your friendship circle and you won't be tardy in offering them.

31 TUESDAY
Moon Age Day 18   Moon Sign Pisces

Be as practical as you like today because it is that side of your personality that is working so well. Although you could find relatives difficult to deal with, in the main you remain sure that you are doing the right thing – although anxious to please. What shows most of all right now is the friendly side of your Aries nature.

August

2018

1 WEDNESDAY   ☿   *Moon Age Day 19   Moon Sign Pisces*

Keep an open mind about inevitable changes at home. Emotional matters are apt to preoccupy you now, which is why you need other matters on which to concentrate from time to time. Don't worry too much about the way those around you are behaving; just as surely as your astrological fortunes fluctuate, so do theirs.

2 THURSDAY   ☿   *Moon Age Day 20   Moon Sign Aries*

The lunar high arrives at the same time as what could be a lull in practical matters so as long as you don't have to work, the time is right for having fun. When it comes to persuading others to join in, you have silver-tongued eloquence right now. Comfort and security are the last things on your agenda today.

3 FRIDAY   ☿   *Moon Age Day 21   Moon Sign Aries*

If this isn't turning out to be a really good time you probably haven't been trying hard enough! You are well ahead of the game in most areas of your life and find yourself in a position from which you can make even more headway. Just make sure that while you are focusing on your ambitious plans, you don't take loved ones for granted.

4 SATURDAY   ☿   *Moon Age Day 22   Moon Sign Taurus*

With the weather likely to be good and the school summer holidays underway, it becomes more important to you to get out and about. You enjoy being in the social mainstream at the moment and so will probably not be concentrating quite as much on practical matters as has been the case during the last couple of weeks.

5 SUNDAY   ☿   *Moon Age Day 23   Moon Sign Taurus*

Protect your interests in some way, even if you have to go to some trouble to do so. It is not a good idea to believe everything you hear today. Although it is unlikely that anyone is deliberately trying to deceive you, you are more easily fooled at the moment than would generally be the case.

6 MONDAY   ☿   *Moon Age Day 24   Moon Sign Gemini*

There is now plenty to occupy your mind, perhaps too much at times. You will certainly gain if you are willing to listen to the help and advice that comes from people who are in the know in any situation. Conforming to expectations may be difficult, but your ideas should benefit from new input as the day advances.

7 TUESDAY   ☿   *Moon Age Day 25   Moon Sign Gemini*

This is a practical, workhorse part of the month and you excel in it, particularly if the spotlight is on you. Comfortable and capable, if some projects have to be broken down into separate tasks you will be more than up to the job of managing and completing them successfully.

8 WEDNESDAY   ☿   *Moon Age Day 26   Moon Sign Gemini*

The planetary focus now is on your strong personality. People are quite happy to defer to you in most situations, just as long as you maintain that air of total self-confidence. Generally speaking, this should be easy, though there are one or two moments today during which you may not be entirely sure of yourself.

9 THURSDAY   ☿   *Moon Age Day 27   Moon Sign Cancer*

The potential for dealing with money-making schemes looks particularly good today, although at the same time you experience some impatience and a desire to put distance between yourself and places you find boring. This wanderlust is set to continue, on and off, for the next three or four weeks at least.

10 FRIDAY ☿ *Moon Age Day 28 Moon Sign Cancer*

Make a special effort now to show that you care, and that your heart is in the right place. In personal relationships, you might have your work cut out today. It is possible that your partner is behaving in a less than typical manner whilst you don't have quite your usual level of patience, which is an unfortunate combination. Try to keep things calm and steady.

11 SATURDAY ☿ *Moon Age Day 0 Moon Sign Leo*

It only takes small alterations in the way you are thinking in order to realise that you are the one in charge. Nothing really changes, but it does make you feel a good deal better. You might otherwise appear to be completely at the behest of other people, possibly because of family commitments and obligations.

12 SUNDAY ☿ *Moon Age Day 1 Moon Sign Leo*

You are ingenious at present and have a number of different schemes in mind. From a social point of view, you welcome the company of interesting and stimulating people, and you mix freely and easily with those you haven't met before. This is also a day when it ought to be easy to make money.

13 MONDAY ☿ *Moon Age Day 2 Moon Sign Virgo*

The mood both at work and at home may be competitive, something from which Aries will not shy away, but the pressure this brings might tire you more quickly than normal. Seek out a complete change of mood at the end of the day. If there are unaccountable setbacks to be dealt with today, you should take these in your stride.

14 TUESDAY ☿ *Moon Age Day 3 Moon Sign Virgo*

In a practical sense, any job you don't particularly relish at the moment ought to be got out of the way early in the day, leaving the decks clear for more pleasurable action. You capitalise well on all offers of social pleasure and at the same time, you know how to make those around you happy.

15 WEDNESDAY ☿   *Moon Age Day 4   Moon Sign Libra*

Prepare for the effects of a planetary lull caused by the lunar low. This comes at a time when you could quite well have done without it. As a result you have a tendency to push forward against insurmountable odds. It would be far better to relax for a couple of days and to see what happens later. Patience really is a virtue today.

16 THURSDAY ☿   *Moon Age Day 5   Moon Sign Libra*

It would be best to keep an open mind about family issues and trust younger people to find their own way through a slightly sticky situation. A little self-indulgence seems in order at the moment. There is nothing you can do to push forward your own interests and you will only become frustrated if you try too hard.

17 FRIDAY ☿   *Moon Age Day 6   Moon Sign Scorpio*

All you really want to do at the start of today is settle back and keep out of the limelight. However, things can soon change in the world of Aries and it won't be long before you are taking more interest in events surrounding you. By the evening, you will hardly remember what the lunar low was.

18 SATURDAY ☿   *Moon Age Day 7   Moon Sign Scorpio*

Put your versatility to good use today and don't be worried about taking on more than one job at a time. Although certain people might think you are running yourself ragged, in reality this is not the case. Don't be afraid to stand up for anyone you think is being maligned or mistreated in any way.

19 SUNDAY   *Moon Age Day 8   Moon Sign Sagittarius*

A domestic matter could prove to be in some way tiring. Take the sting out of its tail by giving more or less all of your time to loved ones today. If this is a quiet Sunday anyway, you will lose very little by relaxing your grip on other matters and, in turn, your attitude will be appreciated and is tantamount to feathering your own nest.

20 MONDAY   *Moon Age Day 9   Moon Sign Sagittarius*

A slight sense of polarisation between work and your home life might mean that you have to split your day somehow. That may not be too easy but it's only a matter of time before you stumble across a sensible compromise that allows you to have your cake and eat it too. Genuine personal contentment may now be achievable.

21 TUESDAY   *Moon Age Day 10   Moon Sign Sagittarius*

A friendship issue may prove to be a letdown, which won't please you very much but try to accept that investing a great deal of confidence in others will occasionally lead to disappointments. However, that's the way you are and getting your fingers burnt now and again will not change your basic attitude – thank goodness.

22 WEDNESDAY   *Moon Age Day 11   Moon Sign Capricorn*

Out there in the social mainstream you do what you can to brighten the middle of the week, both for yourself and for the people you care about the most. Put in that extra little effort to get yourself ahead of the field, and once your position is established it should not be difficult to maintain it.

23 THURSDAY   *Moon Age Day 12   Moon Sign Capricorn*

You enter a go-ahead phase now you should discover some allies you didn't even know you had. You may even be able to persuade someone higher up the tree than you are to give you a helping hand. Almost anything is possible while you are in your present frame of mind and the sky is the limit!

24 FRIDAY   *Moon Age Day 13   Moon Sign Aquarius*

You need to feel fully in charge of every situation today, and problems arise when you discover that doing so isn't so easy. A few people at least seem to be getting in your way and proving to be especially difficult to deal with. Casual conversations can spark off some interesting ideas, particularly with regard to work plans for the near future.

25 SATURDAY   *Moon Age Day 14   Moon Sign Aquarius*

Professionally speaking you ought to be on the up. Of course this depends on whether you work on a Saturday, but if you are not working today try to find some other way to exploit the potential of the day. Avoid family arguments at all costs and make yourself scarce rather than becoming involved in pointless and futile disagreements.

26 SUNDAY   *Moon Age Day 15   Moon Sign Aquarius*

You may feel a great urge to put forward your point of view in a very assertive manner. This is something you really should try to avoid. It may well be the case that you are in the right – but if you are others will soon realise it. Driving the point home aggressively or even dogmatically is more likely to alienate someone.

27 MONDAY   *Moon Age Day 16   Moon Sign Pisces*

There are some fortunate influences around now regarding career prospects. Those Arians who are presently looking for a new job, or between positions, should concentrate their efforts at this time. Some of your personal objectives could become a little muddled while your focus turns elsewhere, but rest assured that they should be sorted soon.

28 TUESDAY   *Moon Age Day 17   Moon Sign Pisces*

Socially speaking, you might be somewhat more reluctant to join the fun than usual. There are a number of small astrological reasons for this state of affairs but none of them are so strong that they cannot be overcome. New contacts are on the cards, together with the chance of meeting pals from the past once again.

29 WEDNESDAY   *Moon Age Day 18   Moon Sign Aries*

Trends place a positive emphasis on the areas of personal security and finances, so a good deal of your time today could be taken up dealing with these matters. There are potential distractions around but it is vitally important that you concentrate. By the evening, you should be registering the fact that romantic prospects are also good.

30 THURSDAY   *Moon Age Day 19   Moon Sign Aries*

With plenty of support coming from your partner or family members, today should be quite happy and generally free from stress. Take the advantage of the lunar high to have a rest, even if resting to you means climbing a mountain or going water skiing. Listen to the advice of a loved one or friend.

31 FRIDAY   *Moon Age Day 20   Moon Sign Aries*

It might be time for a step up the career ladder, and perhaps you are willingly taking on extra responsibilities in the hope that your efforts will be noticed later. You are working hard and putting in that extra bit of effort that can make all the difference, so don't feel deflated if it takes time for this to pay off. Don't be surprised if you are tired by the evening, though.

September

Υ

2018

1 SATURDAY
Moon Age Day 21   Moon Sign Taurus

Today finds you paying particular attention to details in and around your home, but the fact that your chart for this part of September indicates greater movement might also mean your mind is geared towards thoughts of holidays. In general, it is towards the domestic side of life that your mind is apt to turn at the present time.

2 SUNDAY
Moon Age Day 22   Moon Sign Taurus

Take time today to see through to the heart of situations and then to act accordingly. Don't be put off by people who seek to confuse you. Avoid becoming side-tracked by trivia if at all possible. There is so much red tape around, you need to carry a pair of scissors with you, at least in your mind.

3 MONDAY
Moon Age Day 23   Moon Sign Gemini

Although you are busy planning strategies, take time out to have fun or else all the effort is a waste of time. Getting ahead professionally is a means to an end, and not an end in itself. There are some potential high spots in romance this Monday, which many Arians will not want to miss.

4 TUESDAY
Moon Age Day 24   Moon Sign Gemini

Your creative side comes to the fore now, as well as your appreciation for anything artistic or musical and a more considered, cultured Aries is now in evidence. You won't get away with treating people casually today. Demands may be made of you, especially emotional ones, and you have little option but to respond.

5 WEDNESDAY

Moon Age Day 25   Moon Sign Cancer

Don't expect everyone to be on your side at the moment, but when it really matters you should find someone to back you up. Progress at work should come fairly easily if you get the support you need so seek it out – you may discover that it comes from a surprising number of different directions.

6 THURSDAY

Moon Age Day 26   Moon Sign Cancer

Be sure to involve friends in some of your latest enterprises, get out and about when you are not at work and do your best to cheer up the world. That should give you plenty to do! Although you could find yourself feeling rather restless at the moment, this is a state of affairs that you can counter with a little imagination.

7 FRIDAY

Moon Age Day 27   Moon Sign Leo

There are many occasions today when even strangers would lend a hand if they only knew what it was you are after. Your finances should strengthen, especially as you are spending wisely at present. A physical and mental peak arrives for many sons and daughters of Mars. Keep up the pressure and let people know what you want from life.

8 SATURDAY

Moon Age Day 28   Moon Sign Leo

Stand by for a day for some measured risk-taking and for analysing carefully the way events are unfolding for you. Routines are not to your liking because you are clearly making most of the running yourself. It should be easy to pep-up your personal life and to bring about a good deal of excitement in romantic matters.

9 SUNDAY

Moon Age Day 0   Moon Sign Virgo

Socialise when you can and turn your mind to showing your loved ones how important they are to you. Emotions are close to the surface. Don't risk overturning recent successes by being impatient or expecting too much of yourself. A slow and steady sort of Sunday is on offer, which turns out to be no bad thing.

10 MONDAY   *Moon Age Day 1   Moon Sign Virgo*

At work, you have been steaming ahead recently. Now it's time to play and, at present, Aries manages that wonderfully. For the young or young-at-heart amongst you the romantic possibilities of today are pronounced. It isn't so much what you feel for others that counts but more the way you are able to put it into words.

11 TUESDAY   *Moon Age Day 2   Moon Sign Libra*

Avoid complications now and possible pitfalls later by being as truthful and up-front as you can be today. Have fun with cheerful friends. Variety is certainly the spice of life for Aries. Look out for signs of improvements in partnerships, as the Sun continues its stately journey and smiles on you at this time.

12 WEDNESDAY   *Moon Age Day 3   Moon Sign Libra*

Romantic encounters are possible but you simply can't push the issue with anyone at present. However, this is an excellent period for socialising and for bringing your plans to fruition. Mixing business with pleasure could be quite easy and you may get the opportunity to start down a new path towards an alternative form of success.

13 THURSDAY   *Moon Age Day 4   Moon Sign Scorpio*

In terms of money you now need to take a longer-term view and be willing to listen to the timely advice of professional colleagues. Love comes knocking for some Arians later in the day. This is a period during which your desire for material success is extremely well marked, though you should not be too quick to take chances.

14 FRIDAY   *Moon Age Day 5   Moon Sign Scorpio*

Don't allow discussions to turn into arguments, even if you have little or nothing to do with the way they begin. Instead, focus on this as a socially helpful period in which you can enjoy your present popularity, whilst at the same time gently turning casual conversations into concrete ways of getting ahead in life.

15 SATURDAY   *Moon Age Day 6   Moon Sign Scorpio*

The weekend offers a sense of variety when you feel you need it the most, while the potential for romance is extremely strong. What will probably please you most of all is the level of your popularity. In a moment-by-moment sense this could turn out to be one of the most fortunate days of the month for you.

16 SUNDAY   *Moon Age Day 7   Moon Sign Sagittarius*

Try to make this a special day for yourself and everyone you come across. When you're in the right mood, you can be the brightest, happiest and most rewarding person to know. Aries is working at its best now and, true to your sign, those comments you are making cannot be misconstrued by anyone at all.

17 MONDAY   *Moon Age Day 8   Moon Sign Sagittarius*

Don't dwell too much on personal issues just for the moment. It is important to take life slowly, steadily and without too much fuss today. You should find yourself generally content and perhaps less rushed than was the case yesterday. Effort is necessary but you easily get where you want to go.

18 TUESDAY   *Moon Age Day 9   Moon Sign Capricorn*

You continue to get the best from both career and personal matters now. Don't worry too much about details, most of which will take care of themselves. If you feel tired later in the day, be prepared to take a rest and don't push yourself into situations that you don't like the look of.

19 WEDNESDAY   *Moon Age Day 10   Moon Sign Capricorn*

Prepare for some delays in a domestic matter, together with a number of people in your environment making quite excessive demands upon your time. Try to step aside and create a small, private space for yourself. Even Aries needs rest now and again and can't go on pushing ahead at breakneck speed indefinitely.

20 THURSDAY   *Moon Age Day 11   Moon Sign Aquarius*

It is better by far today to pick one job and to do it properly. Some unfavourable planetary trends mean that you can expect your confidence to sag a little, and there probably isn't very much you can do to counter the situation. Simply jog along pleasantly but don't feel that you have to move any mountains.

21 FRIDAY   *Moon Age Day 12   Moon Sign Aquarius*

Try to avoid rash decisions and, if possible, qualify your own thoughts by running them past people you consider to be wise. There are matters in life today that you cannot take for granted, and failure to recognise this may mean that problems dog your footsteps. Look carefully at your actions and think deeply before you make any move.

22 SATURDAY   *Moon Age Day 13   Moon Sign Aquarius*

Contact with people you know well can lead to some interesting possibilities. At home you are creative and anxious to brighten up your surroundings in some way. In any situation that leaves you feeling as though life has been second-rate recently you need to put in that extra bit of effort to lift your spirits.

23 SUNDAY   *Moon Age Day 14   Moon Sign Pisces*

Impatience with specific obligations is part of the package you have to deal with today. You would much rather be giving your time to grandiose new schemes, or perhaps even to some ventures that others would call odd or foolish. If you are really sure of yourself though, you should still follow your own ideas.

24 MONDAY   *Moon Age Day 15   Moon Sign Pisces*

Though you are hardly backsliding professionally you might need some sort of assistance and that means asking for it. In a home-based situation it is possible that you will have to eat some humble pie, never a pleasant experience for you. However, you should feel good once you have taken the plunge.

25 TUESDAY
Moon Age Day 16   Moon Sign Aries

Good fortune follows you around like a friend right now, offering you the chance to get ahead in ways you hadn't expected. People are likely to gather round to lend a hand and this could create an interesting set of circumstances for you. Your immense kindness is clearly on display at this time.

26 WEDNESDAY
Moon Age Day 17   Moon Sign Aries

The planetary picture looks especially good for you right now. Not only are you supported by generally positive planetary trends but you should be extra lucky whilst the lunar high is around. This really is the very best of times to concentrate your efforts and show the world what you are made of.

27 THURSDAY
Moon Age Day 18   Moon Sign Aries

Although today you may enjoy a relaxed phase as far as your personal life is concerned, this probably won't be the case in practical matters. Many people may demand your attention at the same time, leaving you dealing with a dozen jobs and probably getting none of them done adequately. Try to delegate some tasks where you can.

28 FRIDAY
Moon Age Day 19   Moon Sign Taurus

The more independent your approach to life is at present, the greater are likely to be the rewards. Don't be left at the back of the queue at work but push your way forward and insist that your voice is heard. Bear in mind, though, that controlling your own destiny might seem all-important but you can afford to give some ground without losing out in the end.

29 SATURDAY
Moon Age Day 20   Moon Sign Taurus

Some Arians might consider this to be quite a nothing sort of day but if this is the case, you probably are not watching closely enough. It's the things that happen beneath the surface that count the most. When it comes to dealing with people you don't know very well, intuition could be your best guide.

30 SUNDAY
Moon Age Day 21   Moon Sign Gemini

The things that happen today, socially or in a cultural sense could prove to be very important in the weeks to come. This is no time to take your eye off any ball. Although you are generally perceptive right now there is just a slight chance that someone with a very slick approach could fool you.

October

2018

1 MONDAY
Moon Age Day 22   Moon Sign Gemini

You want to create a pleasant environment for everyone and won't take kindly to people who show a desire to upset the applecart in any way. However, it is important to keep your temper and not to allow yourself to rise to any bait that is being deliberately dangled by someone who may not like you very much.

2 TUESDAY
Moon Age Day 23   Moon Sign Cancer

The ability to mix business with pleasure is the great forte of your zodiac sign and this fact really shows today. The accent now is clearly on romance and fun. You can perfect your creative skills in organising gatherings or social functions, whilst at the same time feathering your nest in more practical ways.

3 WEDNESDAY
Moon Age Day 24   Moon Sign Cancer

Although you might feel a great sense of freedom around now, you won't be all that keen to travel further than is strictly necessary. Concentrate today on more emotional or even spiritual matters, since the arrival of this particular Wednesday should bring more time to stand aside from the purely practical aspects of life.

4 THURSDAY
Moon Age Day 25   Moon Sign Leo

New relationships could be on the cards for Arians who have been looking for love and you won't have any difficulty at all charming the birds down from the trees, either now or tomorrow. Romantically and personally, today should mark one of the most enjoyable times during the whole of October.

135

5 FRIDAY
Moon Age Day 26   Moon Sign Leo

Today should find you quite contented. There is a strong sense of togetherness around, which is especially emphasised in your love life today. Relating to people from your past should now also be easier and you might be in a position to bury a hatchet that has been a problem for quite some time. Arbitrating between others is also possible.

6 SATURDAY
Moon Age Day 27   Moon Sign Virgo

Don't let yourself become upset about matters in the wider family, some of which appear to be giving you a slightly hard time today. It is close partnerships that make life most fulfilling now, both in a romantic sense and for those of you who are in co-operative professional ventures. Focus on these areas until tension in others dissipates.

7 SUNDAY
Moon Age Day 28   Moon Sign Virgo

Someone you haven't seen for ages could be visiting your life again today. Listen to what others are saying, especially your life partner. He or she is likely to have some very good ideas at present. These, taken together with your own ability to make reality from fantasy, prove to be extremely important in your life right now.

8 MONDAY
Moon Age Day 29   Moon Sign Virgo

Aries is sometimes accused of being selfish, though the truth is that you are merely single-minded. Having said this, it wouldn't do any harm today to remember that there are other people involved in your decisions. It is possible that you are thinking of number one at the beginning of this working week – and this is never a good idea if it blinds you to those around you.

9 TUESDAY
Moon Age Day 0   Moon Sign Libra

The arrival of the lunar low will probably coincide with a less-active phase that will continue for a couple more days. Be careful whom you trust today. Even though your instincts right now are to give others the benefit of the doubt, there are one or two people around at present that may not be what they seem.

10 WEDNESDAY   *Moon Age Day 1   Moon Sign Libra*

Avoid being too quick to jump to conclusions, and a degree of circumspection would also be sensible. There are advantages to looking at specific situations in isolation around now. This Wednesday brings a desire to spend time with family members and to do something you see as being essentially interesting.

11 THURSDAY   *Moon Age Day 2   Moon Sign Scorpio*

This ought to be a bright and breezy sort of day, without too much in the way of perceived responsibility but with plenty of entertainment and fun. The friendly assistance that comes from the direction of people you know, as well as strangers, is bound to be especially well received today.

12 FRIDAY   *Moon Age Day 3   Moon Sign Scorpio*

It isn't the things you want to do that matter right now but rather the things you have to do. As long as you keep a smile on your face, the day should prove to be a breeze. Professional matters are likely to go more smoothly today, even if in your heart you would rather be somewhere else.

13 SATURDAY   *Moon Age Day 4   Moon Sign Sagittarius*

Not much ruffles your feathers at the moment, though you won't take too kindly to being told what to do. This only really applies if you work on a Saturday. Most home-based situations ought to prove distinctly relaxing, so your main focus today is likely to be on your domestic life. Enjoy the chance to put yourself first for once!

14 SUNDAY   *Moon Age Day 5   Moon Sign Sagittarius*

Perhaps you are slightly more considerate than usual regarding the feelings of those around you. Aries is becoming quite creative around now, perhaps leading to a decorating spree at home. Social and teamwork matters are favourably highlighted now, and these trends suggest that you will be getting on well with the world at large.

15 MONDAY
Moon Age Day 6   Moon Sign Capricorn

Not everything interests you today, but lots will. Getting to know others can be extraordinarily fascinating, particularly when you are dealing with people who have a mysterious fascination of some sort. Along comes a period of high enthusiasm and a time when you are showing your best face to the world at large.

16 TUESDAY
Moon Age Day 7   Moon Sign Capricorn

The impact of your personality remains generally strong, so it isn't hard to get what you want from life, or to influence people along the way. Romance is a possibility, and if you are single this could perhaps be coming from an unexpected direction. Alternatively, an old flame could be rekindled before the weekend.

17 WEDNESDAY
Moon Age Day 8   Moon Sign Capricorn

Although things are getting better and better from a social point of view, they don't maintain the same sort of momentum in material matters or professional situations. Keep it light and simple, that's the recipe for success this Wednesday. Since you are quite lucky under present trends, what about a shopping expedition?

18 THURSDAY
Moon Age Day 9   Moon Sign Aquarius

There is little reason why your plans should fail to materialise more or less the way you have envisaged them. There may be hurdles to overcome, but these are meat and drink to your zodiac sign at the present time. Some slight ill health is indicated for some Arians, though almost certainly of a very minor nature. Wrap up warm if it's cold though!

19 FRIDAY
Moon Age Day 10   Moon Sign Aquarius

It appears that your opinions carry a great deal of weight in the minds of your friends and colleagues. This is a time to show your ingenious nature working at its best. Socially speaking, you can enjoy a fairly easy-going sort of period and may not wish to be involved in lengthy or deep conversations of any sort.

20 SATURDAY
Moon Age Day 11   Moon Sign Pisces

You should be making the most of all social encounters today, particularly ones that have shades of work associated with them. However, trying to think of something different to say to superiors can be a slight difficulty, especially if they are people for whom you have no real personal respect. Make sure you maintain a professional attitude at all times.

21 SUNDAY
Moon Age Day 12   Moon Sign Pisces

If there is any way in which you can spoil yourself, today it is important that you utilise it. Of course you will not forget the responsibility you feel towards others but you can't be on duty all the time. It is important to sort out finances now, particularly those you share with other people.

22 MONDAY
Moon Age Day 13   Moon Sign Pisces

If you box clever and use a little friendly persuasion today, especially at home, you can get people to do more or less whatever you wish. Some slight difficulties could be forthcoming with younger family members but this is really only a case of trying to see things from their point of view.

23 TUESDAY
Moon Age Day 14   Moon Sign Aries

There is now room to grow and to think up interesting new ideas that are going to be extremely useful as this year comes to an end. Mental stimulus coming in from a number of different directions helps to push you forward at this time. Don't be too quick to judge the actions of a relative or a very close friend.

24 WEDNESDAY
Moon Age Day 15   Moon Sign Aries

Things are hotting up again and the presence of the lunar high certainly helps you get ahead. You are now dynamic and raring to have a go at things that you shied away from only a day or two ago. If you want an October day on which it proves possible to move mountains, this could be it.

25 THURSDAY   *Moon Age Day 16   Moon Sign Taurus*

You might find it inspiring to seek out new contacts today, as well as getting a great deal from people who figure prominently in your life. Personal relationships should also be looking good and you have more than a slight chance of getting ahead of the game in the financial stakes.

26 FRIDAY   *Moon Age Day 17   Moon Sign Taurus*

Having moved steadily towards some of your life's goals in the recent past, you now find yourself at some sort of culmination point. That means looking again at issues and deciding where your effort is best concentrated henceforth. A chat with your partner or family members could help.

27 SATURDAY   *Moon Age Day 18   Moon Sign Gemini*

You might be kept in the dark regarding the plan of action that others are laying. It really is up to you to make certain that you are not ignored and that your point of view gets an airing. If this means being even nosier than usual, then so be it. There is also a chance of new personalities entering your life around now.

28 SUNDAY   *Moon Age Day 19   Moon Sign Gemini*

This is an excellent time to broaden your horizons in a general sense but you could also find yourself making a journey to a place of interest. Certainly, finding yourself stuck in any sort of rut has no appeal for you whatsoever. Those Arians who can take a break now are the luckiest of all; even a Sunday drive or walk would be beneficial.

29 MONDAY   *Moon Age Day 20   Moon Sign Cancer*

It is possible that the working week begins with you thinking of number one. As an Aries, you know that this can be a little weakness of yours, especially when it leads you to disregard the feelings of others. Keep in mind today that the planets are bringing this tendency to the fore and take especial care to avoid any negative situations arising from it.

30 TUESDAY   *Moon Age Day 21   Moon Sign Cancer*

A fun and sociable sort of day is on the cards. You can expect to benefit from some help and support from people around you, even those you don't know very well. This will lighten the load of responsibility and enable you to focus on the good times. Make sure you say 'thank you' though!

31 WEDNESDAY   *Moon Age Day 22   Moon Sign Cancer*

In the hustle and bustle of a busy working week, you might fail to notice what is going on at home. That could turn out to be something of a mistake, so find a few moments to check out the feelings of loved ones, especially your partner. Living in a world that only includes you would definitely be a mistake at this time.

♈ *November* 2018

1 THURSDAY
Moon Age Day 23   Moon Sign Leo

Although some goals and ambitions seem a long way off, with a little patience you can start an important personal journey today. In terms of your career, a plan of action may fail to yield the sort of results you would wish. Don't abandon what you have thought up but rather look at things afresh and make some modifications.

2 FRIDAY
Moon Age Day 24   Moon Sign Leo

Working slowly but definitely towards your objectives you ought to be fired up with enthusiasm and quite happy to ring the changes socially. It is at work that the greatest movement begins to show and this continues until the weekend. Significant progress is possible, at least for a day or two.

3 SATURDAY
Moon Age Day 25   Moon Sign Virgo

You have a strong desire to be in the know at the moment and a need to be aware of how and why things work in the way they do. There is much about today that will fascinate you. When it comes to social encounters you are the centre of attraction and can get other people on your side when it proves to be necessary.

4 SUNDAY
Moon Age Day 26   Moon Sign Virgo

There is assistance around if you need it but in the main you are happy to go your own way and won't be held back by insignificant details. Absolute determination is the key to Aries success at present. Today looks as though it will bring plenty of energy and a great deal of determination to get ahead in any way you can.

5 MONDAY
Moon Age Day 27   Moon Sign Libra

Avoid signing documents or making agreements today unless you have read the small print very carefully and be particularly scrupulous in all business dealings. The lunar low could make your professional successes fairly minimal, and yet this is a time during which personal attachments can offer a great deal.

6 TUESDAY
Moon Age Day 28   Moon Sign Libra

In all probability those around you definitely do have your best interests at heart and so calling upon them for any sort of assistance won't be a problem. Romance is also well starred under present trends. It is clear that you are now keen to seek out new horizons and to do what appeals in an adventurous sense.

7 WEDNESDAY
Moon Age Day 0   Moon Sign Scorpio

Following the lunar low this could prove to be one of the best days of November when it comes to career interests. However, do take care to diversify when necessary and don't allow yourself to get stuck in any sort of rut. Listen to some sound professional advice from someone in the know.

8 THURSDAY
Moon Age Day 1   Moon Sign Scorpio

In all probability this will not be the best time for keeping up a high social profile. Although it isn't a common occurrence for you, there is a tendency for you to be quite shy today. Deal with this very temporary phase by concentrating on those things you know to be of importance and leave the social niceties until later.

9 FRIDAY
Moon Age Day 2   Moon Sign Sagittarius

At work you need to show a very positive face to new initiatives, even if you have doubts about them. News from far off should prove to be a good stimulus to your personal life. Maybe someone you haven't heard from for ages is getting in touch again, offering you a journey or the chance to plan one.

10 SATURDAY   *Moon Age Day 3   Moon Sign Sagittarius*

Arians who take a responsible attitude to life will already be planning for Christmas and today would be fine for shopping or for looking carefully at exactly what is available to spend. You may be too busy to think much about money in a day-to-day sense and yet it is very important to do so.

11 SUNDAY   *Moon Age Day 4   Moon Sign Sagittarius*

Creature comforts have slightly less appeal now and you are willing to go without almost anything in the search to get what you really want from life. This would be another favourable time to broaden your horizons, though you probably won't begin doing so until the middle of the day.

12 MONDAY   *Moon Age Day 5   Moon Sign Capricorn*

Loving relationships are quite obvious as a place to go once the working day is over, but trends suggest that the comfort you find there might be marred by certain family members behaving in a less than typical way. Don't allow this to spoil your pleasure in your downtime, as tomorrow you will need to work hard once again.

13 TUESDAY   *Moon Age Day 6   Moon Sign Capricorn*

Today brings a great sense of wonder and a desire to consider all the options, making this a rather special, if somewhat odd, day. As you embark on your personal voyage of discovery, don't be at all surprised if you discover some facts and figures that give you a greater understanding of the way the world works.

14 WEDNESDAY   *Moon Age Day 7   Moon Sign Aquarius*

The active and enterprising side of your nature is on display, at least in a planning sense as, in fact, the activity has to come later. You may not be exactly moving any mountains but you can enjoy yourself in a quiet way and perhaps get to know someone close to you better than has been the case for quite a while.

15 THURSDAY   *Moon Age Day 8   Moon Sign Aquarius*

Concentrate on the matter at hand today, even though trends suggest that this might be quite difficult. When the practicalities are out of the way, make the most of very favourable social and romantic trends. This is an ideal time to decide whether you should jettison some aspects of life that are now of little or no use to you.

16 FRIDAY   *Moon Age Day 9   Moon Sign Aquarius*

Social and teamwork matters are favourably highlighted now, leading to a feeling that you can get on well with just about anyone. Perhaps you are slightly more considerate regarding the feelings of those around you than you are sometimes inclined to be. Take note of the positive reaction that comes from this and store it away for times when you default to a less empathetic frame of mind.

17 SATURDAY   ☿   *Moon Age Day 10   Moon Sign Pisces*

While your ability to concentrate on detailed work could be lacking today, you can make up for this with your enthusiasm for social events, especially if you don't work at the weekend. Don't stress if you can't achieve everything you set out to do but focus on the good mood that the present fun-loving Aries is enjoying.

18 SUNDAY   ☿   *Moon Age Day 11   Moon Sign Pisces*

Trends suggest that right now you are getting your own way in almost everything. It should prove easy to achieve your personal goals and you are drawing closer and closer to a time when you can ease off some of the pressure and gain from the work you put in before. That's not the case yet – but you still have rather a good day in store.

19 MONDAY   ☿   *Moon Age Day 12   Moon Sign Aries*

You start today on a mental and physical peak and won't have very much trouble at all letting others know that you mean business. So good is the impression you are giving that you might be offered some new opportunities. Nobody could fail to register your very positive presence at this stage of the month.

20 TUESDAY ☿ *Moon Age Day 13* *Moon Sign Aries*

The lunar high can set this part of the working week apart, though you will have to put in some effort yourself. If people are reluctant to go along with your plans, try talking them into co-operating. There is very little around to prevent you from getting what you want just now, either personally or professionally.

21 WEDNESDAY ☿ *Moon Age Day 14* *Moon Sign Taurus*

Don't become dominated by negative behavioural patterns. Stick to what you're good at, stay cheerful and make as many jokes as you can. That's the way most people like you to be and it can get you a long way. Conforming to expectations at work might be the most difficult job of all.

22 THURSDAY ☿ *Moon Age Day 15* *Moon Sign Taurus*

Prepare for a fairly average sort of day and don't push your luck too much. It won't be long before you are back on top form again but just for now you have little choice but to settle for second best. Conforming to the expectations that friends have of you could seem tedious but it does help your overall reputation.

23 FRIDAY ☿ *Moon Age Day 16* *Moon Sign Taurus*

Pleasure seeking and self-indulgence appear to be the order of the day. This is fine, but there will come a time when you feel in need of a little introspection. Mixing and mingling the possibilities of this day is what makes it uniquely interesting, but put off tedious jobs that bore you for another day if you can.

24 SATURDAY ☿ *Moon Age Day 17* *Moon Sign Gemini*

Some emotions are very close to the surface at present, particularly at home. This means that you could be rather touchier than would normally be the case. Try to find ways today to enjoy yourself and put some of your responsibilities on the back burner. Trends suggest that family members should be doing their best to be accommodating.

25 SUNDAY ☿ *Moon Age Day 18   Moon Sign Gemini*

Professional objectives need to be handled especially carefully right now. If you are at work today there are possible defeats in view, and you won't take kindly to this at all. Think before you act and if you are in any doubt, don't act at all. If you are not at work, take any chance to be involved in social gatherings that require little from you except your presence.

26 MONDAY ☿ *Moon Age Day 19   Moon Sign Cancer*

It is easy to tell today how many people hold you in high esteem. You could be surprised at the number, particularly if you learn you are popular with a few people you didn't think liked you at all. Don't be slow when it comes to asking for what you want, especially in a material sense.

27 TUESDAY ☿ *Moon Age Day 20   Moon Sign Cancer*

This should prove to be an industrious period, though there might not be much time for enjoyment. Aries is on full alert now and making the most of every opportunity that comes along. But how important is that if you don't manage to have some fun along the way? Balance in everything is the key.

28 WEDNESDAY ☿ *Moon Age Day 21   Moon Sign Leo*

Matters close to your heart are boosted today and that sensitivity, so much on display recently, is now stronger than ever. Not all your wishes come true right now but you should be willing to put in that extra bit of personal effort that will make all the difference. The world might struggle to keep up with you today.

29 THURSDAY ☿ *Moon Age Day 22   Moon Sign Leo*

Your love life should be highly rewarding today so expect some lovely romantic moments. This positive mood makes for another excellent period in this sphere of your life. Generally, you seem to be enjoying a high level of popularity, with people virtually lining up to help you out in any way they can.

30 FRIDAY ☿ *Moon Age Day 23   Moon Sign Virgo*

In terms of progress towards major ambitions this is likely to be a fairly quiet sort of day. That's good, because it means you can concentrate on having fun, in the company of people you care for a great deal. Beware of possible deception, perhaps coming from the direction of someone you once called a friend.

December

2018

1 SATURDAY ☿ *Moon Age Day 24   Moon Sign Virgo*

Aries is extremely innovative at the moment and others would be sensible if they took notice of what you have to say. Friends should be especially attentive. You make your way in life by relying on your own ideas and your ability to think up new concepts – and nothing is different about that situation now.

2 SUNDAY ☿ *Moon Age Day 25   Moon Sign Libra*

If you want a day during which you can make an impact on the world, this is not it. Instead of trying to do everything yourself, allow others to take at least part of the strain. This does not mean you are likely to lose control, so don't get upset about a fairly compulsory layoff that only lasts a couple of days.

3 MONDAY ☿ *Moon Age Day 26   Moon Sign Libra*

Not everyone is going to behave as you might have imagined and you will need some flexibility to cope with this. A charming social performance on your part could impress any number of people. Astrological trends point to a rather unusual start to the week and a time during which you could easily be surprised.

4 TUESDAY ☿ *Moon Age Day 27   Moon Sign Scorpio*

Almost anyone will be pleased to hear what you have to say right now and their reactions could be surprising. All aspects of communication are going extremely well at present. With some entertaining people on the horizon and almost everything going your way, the time has come to put your thoughts into tangible form.

5 WEDNESDAY   ☿   *Moon Age Day 28*   *Moon Sign Scorpio*

Routine is something you would not welcome right now and it is quite obvious that you are up for as much variety in life as you can get. Your energy levels are now plentiful and you will have little or no difficulty in getting what you need from life, even if you cannot manage to get everything you want.

6 THURSDAY   ☿   *Moon Age Day 29*   *Moon Sign Scorpio*

Confidence remains the key and the world marvels at your versatility. Communications work favourably now in order to bring you what you want the most. There may also be a slightly inward-looking tendency developing so that it isn't so much a matter of what you can achieve that counts but rather why.

7 FRIDAY   *Moon Age Day 0*   *Moon Sign Sagittarius*

There is much activity today and, perhaps, a desire to get as much Christmas shopping done as early as you can. Intellectual stimulus is what you really need and you will deliberately be offering yourself up for puzzles of one sort or another. These could be practical in nature or simply for the sake of entertainment.

8 SATURDAY   *Moon Age Day 1*   *Moon Sign Sagittarius*

After a really hectic week you might decide that it's time to simply have some fun and nobody is going to argue with that. Avoid getting involved in a domestic dustup and instead show that you are sweetness and light to everyone. In group or co-operative matters you make certain you are on the winning side.

9 SUNDAY   *Moon Age Day 2*   *Moon Sign Capricorn*

A change of pace would do you the world of good around now. Leave work issues on the back-burner for Sunday at least and concentrate instead on what your social life is presently offering. This may not be the best time of all for starting a new health regime but in the end only you can be the judge.

10 MONDAY   *Moon Age Day 3   Moon Sign Capricorn*

Socially speaking you appear to be on top form and will even be forging alliances with people you haven't necessarily seen eye to eye with in the past. The attitudes and opinions of family members may be quite surprising at times. The opportunity for meeting new people has rarely been better than it is right now.

11 TUESDAY   *Moon Age Day 4   Moon Sign Aquarius*

You have masses of energy and will be able to operate on several different fronts at the same time. There are significant gains in the offing and a chance to show your mettle at exactly the right time. There is something of the warrior about you at the moment and it is very unlikely that you would be settling for second best.

12 WEDNESDAY   *Moon Age Day 5   Moon Sign Aquarius*

Though you may not enjoy quite as much progress as you would wish in the practical world, getting along with others has rarely been easier. With the lunar high not all that far away, you can use present trends to set up meetings for next week. Once work is out of the way, find different ways in which to enjoy yourself.

13 THURSDAY   *Moon Age Day 6   Moon Sign Aquarius*

You should be feeling fairly good about yourself today and it is clear that you are taking a more dominant role at this stage of December. This will be especially true in any sort of family arrangements. Stand by for a crackerjack of a time ahead and one that offers much in the way of change.

14 FRIDAY   *Moon Age Day 7   Moon Sign Pisces*

A period of potential financial improvement is at hand. This is obviously a positive thing so close to Christmas. Part of the situation depends upon you looking carefully at your own money, and seeing how you can rationalise some spending. In the end you should find yourself better off than you thought.

15 SATURDAY   *Moon Age Day 8   Moon Sign Pisces*

The emphasis you wish to place on material and professional plans now receives a very definite boost. Make an early start and you should find you get on top of things quickly. Routines are definitely out at present as you move forward positively into areas of life that fascinate you.

16 SUNDAY   *Moon Age Day 9   Moon Sign Pisces*

The more settled amongst you will be consolidating personal attachments and finding moments to say those little words that are most important. Family-motivated interests probably dominate as Christmas approaches. Trends also suggest that a social contact could develop into something much more if you are an Aries who is open to new romance.

17 MONDAY   *Moon Age Day 10   Moon Sign Aries*

New avenues of communication tend to open up during this, the most potentially interesting of times. Although it might sometimes be further to the winning post that you might have imagined, it's worth keeping on running in almost any situation. Success can be truly yours with only a modicum of effort now.

18 TUESDAY   *Moon Age Day 11   Moon Sign Aries*

There is more than a small element of luck attending anything you undertake now and the lunar high helps you in other ways too. Romance is high on your agenda and some Arians will notice that potential affection is not simply coming from expected directions. You are simply very attractive at present.

19 WEDNESDAY   *Moon Age Day 12   Moon Sign Taurus*

Don't be surprised if certain career issues and opportunities make themselves known at this stage of the week, immediately ahead of the Christmas break. There isn't much you can do about them now and by the middle of the day your thought will almost certainly have turned in a less practical and a more seasonal direction.

20 THURSDAY   *Moon Age Day 13   Moon Sign Taurus*

Social meetings and talks of various kinds should be highly rewarding. There is much good humour about and with Christmas just around the corner, it's clear that you are out to enjoy yourself as much as you can. Don't overtax your mind in terms of practical matters – today you need to party.

21 FRIDAY   *Moon Age Day 14   Moon Sign Gemini*

The trends around now are slightly unhelpful when it comes to general communication. If someone seems rather critical of either your attitude or approach, simply ignore what they have to say and get on with your own life. There is no point in reacting to situations you can't alter. A cheerful attitude is everything today.

22 SATURDAY   *Moon Age Day 15   Moon Sign Gemini*

It may not be quite as simple to get through to people today as you might have expected. It doesn't matter if you have to explain yourself two, or even three times. What remains important is to ensure that those closest to you understand perfectly what you are trying to tell them. For once you show supreme patience.

23 SUNDAY   *Moon Age Day 16   Moon Sign Cancer*

Test your luck today because it is highly unlikely to let you down. Routines could be something of a bind, so avoid them altogether if you possibly can. Meanwhile you push forward progressively and will already have begun the round of parties and enjoyment that means Christmas to you.

24 MONDAY   *Moon Age Day 17   Moon Sign Cancer*

A romantic offer could be coming your way, particularly if you have been searching for new beginnings. Your confidence is generally high at the moment though you will have your work cut out keeping all the balls in the air that you are juggling right now. Don't forget, Christmas is only a day away.

25 TUESDAY
Moon Age Day 18   Moon Sign Leo

On Christmas Day the planets are working well for you, a fact that brings a high degree of warmth to the festivities as far as you are concerned. Close attachments are the most memorable at this time, whilst getting on side with younger people turns out to be much easier than you thought. A happy and satisfying day is in prospect.

26 WEDNESDAY
Moon Age Day 19   Moon Sign Leo

Boxing Day could be a great time for gathering new information, as well as for interpreting the facts and figures of life in quite a new way. You won't be unduly stressed at present, though one or two family members could be. Try to offer the help you can and provide a listening ear.

27 THURSDAY
Moon Age Day 20   Moon Sign Virgo

There is likely to be a great deal of coming and going today, so much so that you might find it difficult to actually concentrate on anything at all. Maybe that's no bad thing. Specifics are not what your life is about right now and a little guesswork is part of the present Aries way to success.

28 FRIDAY
Moon Age Day 21   Moon Sign Virgo

Stand by for an advantageous period financially and to discover a new way to build up your personal fortune. This looks likely to develop over the weeks and months ahead but the process begins now. You strike a good balance between spending and saving, together with some important new ideas that are going to work well for you.

29 SATURDAY
Moon Age Day 22   Moon Sign Libra

Those around you might be surprised at your tendency to avoid too much alcohol or rich food. Still, you will be content and happy with your lot and in a position to offer much support to family members and friends. Trends suggest that you may not feel any particular drive to push yourself forward or to live the high life.

30 SUNDAY
Moon Age Day 23   Moon Sign Libra

If you feel rather out of sorts right now, blame the fact that the Moon is in your opposite zodiac sign. At least you get this interlude out of the way before the New Year celebrations and generally have positive influences ahead of you for the remainder of the month. All that is required at the moment is some patience.

31 MONDAY
Moon Age Day 24   Moon Sign Libra

Any resolutions for the year ahead could include a determination to push your practical capabilities to the full. You will want to be noticed today as the lunar low fades and should go to great lengths to make sure that you are not ignored by anyone. Beware of alienating others by adopting an attitude they cannot understand.

155

RISING SIGNS FOR ARIES

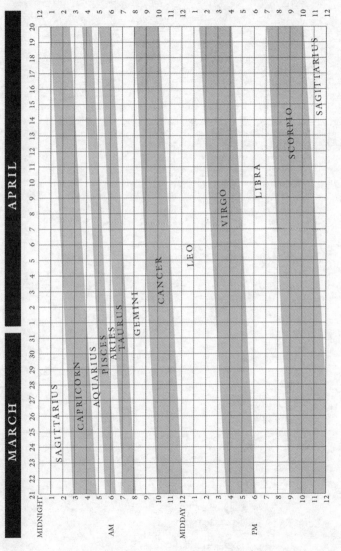

THE ZODIAC, PLANETS AND CORRESPONDENCES

The Earth revolves around the Sun once every calendar year, so when viewed from Earth the Sun appears in a different part of the sky as the year progresses. In astrology, these parts of the sky are divided into the signs of the zodiac and this means that the signs are organised in a circle. The circle begins with Aries and ends with Pisces.

Taking the zodiac sign as a starting point, astrologers then work with all the positions of planets, stars and many other factors to calculate horoscopes and birth charts and tell us what the stars have in store for us.

The table below shows the planets and Elements for each of the signs of the zodiac. Each sign belongs to one of the four Elements: Fire, Air, Earth or Water. Fire signs are creative and enthusiastic; Air signs are mentally active and thoughtful; Earth signs are constructive and practical; Water signs are emotional and have strong feelings.

It also shows the metals and gemstones associated with, or corresponding with, each sign. The correspondence is made when a metal or stone possesses properties that are held in common with a particular sign of the zodiac.

Finally, the table shows the opposite of each star sign – this is the opposite sign in the astrological circle.

Placed	Sign	Symbol	Element	Planet	Metal	Stone	Opposite
1	Aries	Ram	Fire	Mars	Iron	Bloodstone	Libra
2	Taurus	Bull	Earth	Venus	Copper	Sapphire	Scorpio
3	Gemini	Twins	Air	Mercury	Mercury	Tiger's Eye	Sagittarius
4	Cancer	Crab	Water	Moon	Silver	Pearl	Capricorn
5	Leo	Lion	Fire	Sun	Gold	Ruby	Aquarius
6	Virgo	Maiden	Earth	Mercury	Mercury	Sardonyx	Pisces
7	Libra	Scales	Air	Venus	Copper	Sapphire	Aries
8	Scorpio	Scorpion	Water	Pluto	Plutonium	Jasper	Taurus
9	Sagittarius	Archer	Fire	Jupiter	Tin	Topaz	Gemini
10	Capricorn	Goat	Earth	Saturn	Lead	Black Onyx	Cancer
11	Aquarius	Waterbearer	Air	Uranus	Uranium	Amethyst	Leo
12	Pisces	Fishes	Water	Neptune	Tin	Moonstone	Virgo